Early praise for *Developing for Apple Watch, Second Edition*

Often with a new technology, the first books are just retreads of the official docs for years until developers dig into the APIs. With Jeff Kelley having taken that step for us already by working on some of the first shipping WatchKit apps, we get a huge head start. His book is deeply rooted in hard-won lessons about what actually works on Apple Watch, and he shows how to make apps that can really shine on this new platform.

➤ **Chris Adamson**
Author of *iOS 9 SDK Development* and Software Engineer, Rev.com

This is an essential book for any iOS developer interested in getting started with WatchKit. It starts you off with a detailed summary of all of the Apple Watch features and capabilities, and then progresses along a logical path to advanced concepts and performance strategies. Working through each chapter, I started to develop several potential app and app-compliment ideas. I'll be referring to this book often in the near future.

➤ **Kevin J. Garriott**
Director, Mobile Technology, Rockfish

Apple Watch development is new and evolving territory, and this book covers all the bases. If you want to tackle watchOS development, the information you need to fire on all pistons is right here.

➤ **Kevin Munc**
Senior iOS Developer, Method Up LLC

Get energized to develop for the Apple Watch with this book, and learn from an expert!

➤ **Mayur S Patil**
   Assistant Professor, MIT Academy of Engineering, Maharashtra Academy of Engineering and Education Research, Alandi D, Pune

This book does a clear job of going through Apple Watch development in a linear fashion. It will serve as an informative reference for any developer, due to its nicely segmented topics and excellent code examples.

➤ **Jason Humphries**
   Lead iOS Engineer, WedPics

This book tells you how to decide what to build for an Apple Watch and guides you through the whole development.

➤ **Gábor László Hajba**
   IT Consultant, EBCONT Enterprise Technologies GmbH

Developing for Apple Watch, Second Edition

Create Native watchOS 2 Apps with the WatchKit SDK

Jeff Kelley

The Pragmatic Bookshelf

Dallas, Texas • Raleigh, North Carolina

Many of the designations used by manufacturers and sellers to distinguish their products are claimed as trademarks. Where those designations appear in this book, and The Pragmatic Programmers, LLC was aware of a trademark claim, the designations have been printed in initial capital letters or in all capitals. The Pragmatic Starter Kit, The Pragmatic Programmer, Pragmatic Programming, Pragmatic Bookshelf, PragProg and the linking *g* device are trademarks of The Pragmatic Programmers, LLC.

Every precaution was taken in the preparation of this book. However, the publisher assumes no responsibility for errors or omissions, or for damages that may result from the use of information (including program listings) contained herein.

Our Pragmatic courses, workshops, and other products can help you and your team create better software and have more fun. For more information, as well as the latest Pragmatic titles, please visit us at *https://pragprog.com*.

The team that produced this book includes:

Rebecca Gulick (editor)
Potomac Indexing, LLC (index)
Linda Recktenwald (copyedit)
Gilson Graphics (layout)
Janet Furlow (producer)

For customer support, please contact *support@pragprog.com*.

For international rights, please contact *rights@pragprog.com*.

Printed in the United States of America.
ISBN-13: 978-1-68050-133-9
Printed on acid-free paper.
Book version: P1.0—May 2016

Contents

Acknowledgments

The more books I write, the more I appreciate those around me who help me do it.

This book never would have been finished without the continued efforts of Rebecca Gulick, my editor, and the entire staff at The Pragmatic Bookshelf. Their questions, comments, and editing shaped the book into what it is today. Along the same lines, I owe a great deal of thanks to the tech reviewers who helped go over pre-release versions of the book: Chris Adamson, Thomas Alvarez, Albert Choy, Kevin Garriott, Gábor László Hajba, Alexander Henry, Jason Humphries, Carlos Lopez, Kevin Munc, Stephen Orr, Mayur Patil, Kim Shrier, Mario Tatis, Mattio Valentino, Matthew White, and Stephen Wolff. Thanks to them taking time out of their busy schedules, the book's technical contents are that much more accurate.

Working on a book necessarily means not doing other things, and my family has definitely had to put up with my absence and distraction as I've undertaken writing this one. They've earned many thanks. Hopefully watchOS 3 won't change as much as watchOS 2 did!

Finally, I'd like to thank my coworkers and the cofounders of Detroit Labs. Working at such an amazing place allows me to do things like write books in my free time. I can honestly say Detroit Labs is the best place I've ever worked, and I can't imagine being anywhere else.

Preface

Apple Watch has inspired a brand-new platform, watchOS, for iOS develop-ers—that's you!—to take advantage of. You're now competing not only for your users' iPhone screens but also for space on their wrists. For the first time, you can make an iOS app that your users will actually *wear*. As intimate as that is, you want to make sure you can deliver the best experience possible so your app will stay on those wrists. This book will help you make an app that not only stays on your users' wrists, but that they use every single time they look at their watch.

What's in This Book?

This book guides you through the process of creating an Apple Watch app. You'll learn about the kinds of apps you can make for the device, features available to you, and development paradigms you'll use as a watch app developer. By the end of this book, you'll be able to create engaging, full-fea-tured apps for the watch that also interface with their companion iPhone apps, joining forces to create amazing experiences for your users. Here's a quick rundown of what you'll learn in each chapter:

Chapter 1: An Overview of Apple Watch In this chapter you'll learn the basics of the watch: what it can do, what apps on it are like, and how to decide which features of your iPhone app to bring along to your watch app.

Chapter 2: WatchKit Extension Overview A WatchKit extension is where your watch app code will live, and this chapter covers what WatchKit extensions are, how they relate to iPhone apps, and how to test them on real devices.

Chapter 3: WatchKit User Interfaces This chapter dives into the various user-interface (UI) elements available to you on Apple Watch. You'll learn what they are, how to use them, and the layout system that positions them onscreen. You'll also start *TapALap*, the example app we'll create together.

Chapter 4: Organizing Your UI with Groups Expanding on your understanding of the UI layout system that began in Chapter 3, this chapter shows you *groups,* a way to achieve even more complicated and appealing designs in your app.

Chapter 5: Delivering Dynamic Content with Tables This chapter introduces you to *tables*—interface objects you can use to display lists of content to your users. You'll learn how to create them, how to fill them with data, and how to respond to user interaction with them.

Chapter 6: Navigating Between Interfaces You'll compose your watch apps with many screens of content; therefore, a successful app needs to transition from one screen to another. This chapter shows you how, why, and when to move your app to new screens.

Chapter 7: WatchKit Extension Lifecycle At the heart of any watchOS 2 app is the WatchKit extension. In this chapter you'll learn about the proper care and feeding for a WatchKit extension to unlock powerful functionality and become a best-in-class watch app.

Chapter 8: Communicating with WatchConnectivity No app these days is complete without networking, so this chapter shows you how to send and receive data from outside your watch app. Whether you're talking to a server on the Internet or just to your companion iPhone app, you'll learn how to extend your app's reach beyond the wrist.

Chapter 9: Creating Complications with ClockKit Building a watch app that users launch is cool. You know what's cooler? Building an app that shows up on their watch face every time they so much as *look* at their watch. The extra features on the watch face are called *complications,* and this chapter will teach you how to make your own.

Chapter 10: Extending Complications with Time Travel Complications are a deep topic, so this chapter picks up where the previous one left off to cover time travel—showing information about the past and future—in your complications, as well as animations between them!

Chapter 11: Getting Personal with Sensor Data and HealthKit The Apple Watch includes a host of onboard sensors, and this chapter will teach you how to take advantage of them. We'll also use HealthKit to activate the heart rate monitor and use it to track a workout!

Chapter 12: Unlocking Watch App Performance The most useful watch app in the world with the cleanest, most amazing user interface is useless if it can't load before the watch screen deactivates. This chapter will show you all kinds of tips and tricks to maximize the performance of your app.

Chapter 13: Being a Good Watch App Citizen If there's one thing Apple Watch customers appreciate, it's attention to detail. This chapter will show you how to make a watch app that respects all users' physical and mental abilities, speaks to them in their native language, and uses the units of measure they're comfortable with. By doing that, you'll have achieved the final bit of spit and polish for an amazing watchOS app experience.

Who's This Book For?

Making an Apple Watch app, at least for now, means making an iPhone app to contain it. This book assumes some familiarity with making iPhone apps; you should know the basic concepts behind object-oriented programming and be able to follow along with code written in Swift for iOS. Many of the concepts in WatchKit are brand new to even the most experienced iOS developer, so don't worry; I'll explain the code we're writing as we go along.

If you've never made an iOS app before and want to make an amazing iPhone app to go along with your amazing Apple Watch app, the Pragmatic Bookshelf has your back with *iOS 9 SDK Development.*[1] If you're just starting out, I highly recommend reading that book in addition to this one; many of the skills you learn in one will transfer to the other.

The Code in This Book

The code in this book is 100% Swift. While it's still a young language, Swift is clearly the direction in which Apple wants to move, so rather than trying to do both Swift and Objective-C and succeeding at neither, I elected to do this all in one language. The aforementioned book is *also* in Swift, so it serves as a great introduction to iOS in general and Swift specifically.

Now, Swift is a language that's always changing, so it's possible that things will break as new versions of Xcode come out. Fortunately, as a registered Pragmatic Bookshelf customer, you're in luck! I'll be keeping the book up to date and you'll be notified whenever we release an update. As of this writing, the current version of Xcode is 7.2.1, targeting iOS 9.2 and watchOS 2.1. If that seems hilariously old to you, then it's pretty likely that the syntax of Swift has changed. Xcode has some support for bringing things forward into new versions, so try using it to help. If you get stuck, let us know on the book's forum or errata page. More on those next.

---

1. https://pragprog.com/book/adios3/ios-9-sdk-development

Although a later chapter in this book will discuss localization and internationalization for watchOS apps, the majority of the content in this book is in English with units of measure and formatting to American norms. Readers in other countries may need to enter slightly different values in some cases—for instance, entering "0,35" instead of "0.35" for a value in Xcode.

Online Resources

The book's website has links to an interactive discussion forum as well as a place to submit errata for the book.[2] You'll also find links to download the source code for the sample app you'll be working on as you read this book. If you're reading this in ebook form, you'll notice a box above code excerpts that you can click or tap to download the code directly.

Now that we've gotten these things out of the way, your tour through Apple Watch development can begin. Let's start by discussing the device itself, its capabilities and limitations, and what kind of apps you'll want to make for the watch.

---

2. https://www.pragprog.com/titles/jkwatch2

CHAPTER 1

An Overview of Apple Watch

Why a whole chapter on the watch itself? I'm not trying to sell you one. But by understanding more about the device, you'll be able to make smart decisions about the types of apps you should be writing in the first place. In this chapter you'll learn about the fundamental design elements of apps that run on the watch and what your users expect of them. Maybe you're coming to this book thinking you want to make an app for the watch but aren't sure what kind; this chapter will help you brainstorm your app idea. By the end you'll be able to clearly define what the watch can do and, more importantly, what your app inside the watch *should* do.

Apple Watch Basics

Every Apple Watch *must* be paired with an iPhone 5 or newer in order for you to install apps. While a cynic might see this as a sneaky way for Apple to double up on device sales, there's a very good reason: every watchOS app needs to be bundled inside an iOS app that's installed on the iPhone. With the limited screen real estate of the watch, Apple can't exactly have an independent App Store on the device; instead, you'll use the iPhone's Apple Watch app to install new apps.

To know what kinds of apps you can make, it's important to understand the design language of Apple Watch apps. The building blocks you'll use to make the apps are extremely different from the components available to you on iOS. You'll find an entire chapter devoted to the interface components you can use, but a brief overview of what watch apps *look like* is a good place to start brainstorming ideas. Let's begin there.

Apple Watch App-Design Concepts

Much like an iPhone app, you can think of the content of your Apple Watch app one screen at a time, but, of course, the watch screen is much smaller. Here you see an example of a screen you might design for a stopwatch feature.

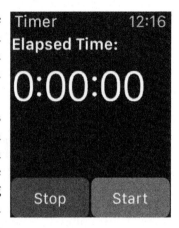

Every screen on Apple Watch automatically scrolls vertically to fit content that exceeds the screen size; the user can either pan with a finger or turn the *Digital Crown*, a grooved button on the side of the watch that rotates to accommodate scrolling and other user input, much like a crown on a traditional wristwatch. Each screen can have a title at the top, tinted to match your app's main color. A stark black background is common, though you *can* change it. Then there are two labels, followed by some buttons. Because of the small screen size, buttons take up a large portion of the screen. You may notice that they go edge to edge, and that's intentional. The bezel of the device adds a black border to every screen, and the margin on the edges is built in, so your designs should stretch as far as possible. The background color of the buttons helps them stand out—bold colors look great on the watch screen.

This is just one screen, and your app will have many. Organizing them is simple, as we'll discuss in a later chapter about transitioning between them. The most common way to have many screens in one app is to use a paged layout. Page-indicator dots at the bottom will inform your users that they can swipe between screens, giving them quick access to all of your features.

When the user presses the screen a bit harder than with a normal tap (called a *Force Touch* in Apple parlance), you can display a contextual menu with additional actions. This is a good place for less-common actions that you want to make available in your app but that you don't necessarily want to take up screen space for. They look like the screen shown here.

One thing you'll notice is that the colors of the app below show through. This transparency (a key element of iOS 7's redesign) is apparent in

Apple Watch apps as well, giving the user a sense of spatial awareness as your app moves from screen to screen.

As you'll see, you can implement many user-interface elements (including images) to create amazing interfaces on these small screens.

From iPhone App to Apple Watch App

When the iPhone SDK came out in 2008, developers struggled to find the right balance. They had Mac apps with tons of great features, but not all of those features made sense on iPhones of the time. Apple gave some guidance, suggesting to developers that they aggressively pare down their apps' feature sets in the transition from OS X to iOS. As time went on, iOS apps became more full-featured than those initial apps, especially with the introduction of the iPad, but OS X apps are still, by nature, more complex.

The Apple Watch and its WatchKit SDK bring us to another such point in time. Not every single feature makes sense to bring from your iPhone app to its WatchKit extension, and some just flat out don't belong. If your app is an RSS reader, for instance, your users aren't going to be reading long-form think pieces on their wrists during their morning commute; they'll just pull out their iPhones for that. That doesn't mean that an RSS reader shouldn't have a WatchKit extension, though—users might want to skim headlines on their watches, saving interesting ones to their reading lists or marking uninteresting articles as read. Other app types might want to bring every feature to the watch if every feature makes sense. So the question is how you pare down the features of an existing iPhone app to those that make sense on the watch.

Finding the Right Features

Think about your app in the context of the watch. Do you have features that would excel on a smaller screen? Quick, easy-to-navigate pieces of information are key here. If your app does light messaging, an inbox is a perfect addition to it. If your app is an RSS reader, on the other hand, full-length feeds aren't as compelling. Focus your effort on the parts of your app that can save your users time—that's why they bought the watch in the first place.

Often, it's a good idea to incorporate only the best-fitting part of your app's features in the watch app. If your app allows its users to change the temperature in their homes as well as schedule recurring temperature changes, consider showing only the controls for adjusting the current temperature.

Since you know users can do more advanced changes on their iPhones, it's a great way to focus and make a more streamlined interface.

After the watch's announcement, you may have started to consider using the device's hardware capabilities. It has a microphone for Siri, an accelerometer, and a heart rate sensor. While the first version of WatchKit didn't include access to any of this hardware, apps built for watchOS 2 can take full advantage of these hardware features and use them to create more engaging apps. You're not limited to simple taps and finger gestures on the watch, so get creative!

Integrating Important Watch Features

A simple messaging app could definitely be ported to WatchKit without losing features, but one feature in particular could make all the difference in the world: actionable notifications. Instead of just showing a user that she has a new message, the developer of a messaging app could create an actionable notification with the option to reply. Now the user doesn't even have to be using that watch app to get value out of it. When the message comes in, she hits Reply, dictates a response, and sends it. This is one of the watch's real strengths: it allows the user to spend the minimum amount of time doing something. Instead of digging out her phone and opening the app to respond, she just needs to move her wrist a little. More on actionable notifications in a later chapter.

Sometimes, despite your watch app's best efforts, users will need to do something on their iPhones. Suppose you have an app for ordering cake to be delivered. On the watch, the user can select a cake to order, pick which color frosting, and even dictate a short phrase to be written on top of the cake. Sounds delicious! But then she goes to place the order and notices that her delivery address is the apartment she just moved out of. Now she's stuck; she just used the watch to make these selections, but without a keyboard on the watch, it's going to be tough to enter a new address. This is a job for Handoff.

Handoff is a feature of both iOS and OS X that allows your app to tell your user's other devices what she's doing. For more information on Handoff, read the Handoff Programming Guide.[1] You describe the *type* of activity the user is engaged in, and the system displays an icon for this activity on the iOS

---

1. https://developer.apple.com/library/ios/documentation/UserExperience/Conceptual/Handoff (In the event this URL is broken on Apple's website in the future, search the iOS developer library for "Handoff.")

lock screen. In the cake example, you'd describe the user's activity as "ordering a cake" and include with it information about the cake that she entered on the watch. From there, the user would open the app on her iOS device through the Handoff icon on the lock screen, and the app would open directly to the cake-ordering screen, allowing the user to change the delivery address to her new apartment and get her cake ordered successfully.

Even though the user in this scenario isn't able to do *everything* on the watch, it's important to save her work so she doesn't feel like it's a waste. In that same scenario *without* Handoff, the user would need to start over on her iPhone, selecting the cake she wants from scratch. By making the user redo everything, you run the risk of alienating her from using the watch app; after all, if she might have to redo it, why not just start on the iPhone?

Providing Information at a Glance

When an Apple Watch user swipes up on the watch face, she sees a list of Glances. A Glance is a miniature version of a watch app; it's one screen of content that she can access quickly, without even opening your watch app. To that end, think about the information in your app that's the most timely to the user: her next meeting, the boarding pass for her flight, or her friends with birthdays today. Put that information in your Glance. When the user taps it, she can go *right* to that piece of information in your watch app, giving her a shortcut to something she needs to access quickly.

Making It Beautiful

Once you know what features you're going to implement in your WatchKit extension and its Glance, put on your designer hat (or hire a designer) and think about your app's user interface. Apple strongly recommends having a dark background. Though Apple hasn't said as much officially, common wisdom suggests that the OLED screens in the watch use less power for black pixels than for white. Since battery life is paramount for the watch, black backgrounds are a good idea. Having said that, color is one of the best ways to make your branding consistent between iPhone and Apple Watch. Try to avoid a black screen full of plain, white labels and stock buttons. Avoid a stark white background, too: be bold with your color choices and try to make your app stand out from the crowd, but aim for color as a highlight on top of a dark background.

Animations are among the coolest things you can do on the watch. Some animations on the watch are simply image sequences, animating like a flip-book. If you can't display a screen immediately—if you need to go out to the network, for instance—use an image sequence animation to indicate that. If a button begins a long-running task like charging a battery, you can add an animation to indicate that's happening. In a small way it can make an otherwise-boring app lively and fresh. Other animations can move user interface elements around, fade them in or out, and perform other small tasks to spice up the app a little.

Wrap-Up

With this introduction to Apple Watch and WatchKit, you now have a better understanding of what kinds of apps you can make for the watch. In the rest of this book we'll go from an idea to a fully featured watch app. First, we'll go over some things you can do in your iPhone app today to work with Apple Watch, even if you don't have your own watch app yet.

WatchKit Extension Overview

Now that you've learned about the watch and what it can do, how do you actually get your app *on* it? You want your app's icon on your users' Apple Watches, and to do that you need a *WatchKit extension.* Why an extension and not just an app? Apple Watch apps (for now) need to exist as a part of their companion iPhone app primarily for distribution—when users install the iPhone app on their phones, they'll be able to install the watch app on their watches. This will add an app icon to their home screen, and from there they can move the icon around, launch the app at will, and show it off to their friends. By bundling the watch app and iPhone app, Apple circumvents the problem of having an App Store on the watch by using the App Store on the phone. So, since you know you'll need to create a WatchKit extension, let's get started!

Creating Your First WatchKit Extension

The traditional first task in any development environment is the ubiquitous "Hello, World!" example. For an Apple Watch app, a good "Hello, World!" will get some text on the screen and react to a button being tapped, so let's start there. Open Xcode and create a new Xcode project by selecting File → New → Project. From the left column under watchOS, select Application, and then select the iOS App with WatchKit App template and click Next. For the name of the project, let's use HelloWatch. Next, Xcode wants an organization name and identifier. What should you use? The answer depends on how you want to test the app.

The examples in this book will use the organization name The Pragmatic Bookshelf with the identifier com.pragprog for these project settings, as shown in the following figure. If you want to test on a real Apple Watch, which we'll go over later, you'll need to use a unique identifier—only one Apple developer account can use the identifier com.pragprog.HelloWatch, and I've already claimed it.

For this project, I've used HelloWatch as the name and com.pragprog as the identifier, so the app's bundle identifier is com.pragprog.HelloWatch. That will come in handy when it's time to do the code signing. With these values set, make sure that the language is set to Swift—this app's source code will be Swift only. Uncheck all of the check boxes underneath the language selection and click Next. Choose a location to save the project and click Create. Just like that, you have a watch app!

 Joe asks:
Can I Hit "Build and Run" Yet?

Sure! But depending on your Xcode configuration, you might be surprised. The list of simulated devices in Xcode may not have any devices paired with a simulated Apple Watch. If you don't see any simulators as a destination when you choose the HelloWatch WatchKit App scheme, you may need to create a new device. To do that, open Xcode's Devices window by clicking Window → Devices or pressing ⌘⇧2. Your list of devices will appear in the left column. Click the + at the bottom-left corner of the window to add a new device. Choose an iPhone 5 or later as the device, and you'll be able to choose an Apple Watch size to go with it. Click Create, and your new device will appear in the Devices window, as well as a destination for the watch app scheme.

Adding User Interface Elements

If you select the watch app target's scheme in Xcode (by clicking HelloWatch in the toolbar and selecting HelloWatch WatchKit App, or selecting Product → Scheme → HelloWatch WatchKit App) and then you build and run (by pressing ⌘R), you'll be greeted with a mostly blank Apple Watch screen with the time in the upper-right corner and nothing else. Congratulations: your first watch app is up and running! Now, let's make it do something. You'll add a button and a label to this screen; tapping the button will change the title of the label. Head to the watch app's storyboard file in Xcode. If you don't see it, open the Project Navigator by pressing ⌘1 and expanding the HelloWatch WatchKit App group; it's named Interface.storyboard. Once you've opened the storyboard, find Xcode's Object Library (^⌥⌘3). Inside the Object Library you'll see everything you can add to your watch app's UI. Let's drag out a button into the black box that appears in the canvas area—the one with the arrow pointing to it. Drop in the button, and it'll snap to the top. Do the same for a label, and it'll snap in underneath the button. That's it! Your UI should look like this.

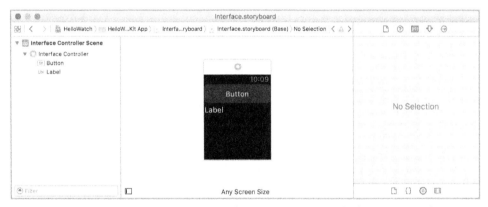

Let's do something more complicated. You're going to link these UI elements to your code, starting with the button, so that tapping the button has an effect in your app. You want to call a method in your code when the user taps the button, at which time you'll change the text of the label. Open the InterfaceController.swift file and add a buttonPressed() function, as follows:

Chapter 2/HelloWatch/HelloWatch WatchKit Extension/InterfaceController.swift

```
@IBAction func buttonPressed() {
    label.setText("Hello, Watch!")
}
```

The code won't build because label isn't defined, so let's fix that. Add a property declaration for it to the InterfaceController class:

```
@IBOutlet var label: WKInterfaceLabel!
```

The code compiles just fine, but if you build and run, nothing works. What gives? Well, you need to link up the interface objects you created earlier with the code you wrote. Just as you would with your iPhone app, you do this in the storyboard. Head back to it and click the black area you've been adding objects to (see an illustrated example of this process in the following figure). Above the black area is a title bar that will contain either an icon or a name. Hold your cursor over the icon, and it will display an *Interface Controller* tooltip. We'll go into more detail on interface controllers later, but for now, just know that this is the object you added your code to. Control-drag from the icon to the label, and then select label under Outlets in the pop-up dialog that appears, as shown here. Control-drag from the button to the icon, and select buttonPressed under Sent Actions. Now your code knows what the label is and what to do when you tap the button. Build and run again, and tap the button. Your first WatchKit app with code you wrote is running! If you have an Apple Watch and want to see it running on the device, skip ahead to the section on deploying to devices, on page 13, and set up your development profile for it.

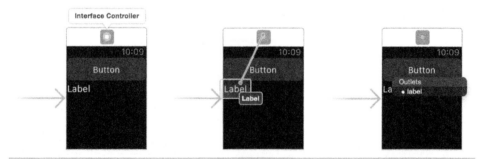

Figure 1—Selecting an outlet for the interface controller in HelloWatch

Adding a Glance

As you learned earlier, on page 5, each watch app can have one Glance to display information to the user right from the watch face. To add one to HelloWatch, open the project in Xcode and open its Interface.storyboard file. In the Object Library in the lower right (available by pressing ⌃⌥⌘3), find the Glance Interface Controller object, and drag it onto the canvas. You'll notice it's full of interface objects, roughly organized into sections. We will discuss these sections, called *groups*, more later in their own chapter, but it's important to note that there are two sections to the Glance, upper and lower.

The Glance interface controller is pretty unique in that you can't directly control its child objects. Try to delete one of the labels, and you'll see that you can't! Similarly, you can't drag new objects onto it from the Object Library. Don't despair, however; a modicum of customization is still available to you. Select the Glance interface controller and open the Attributes Inspector in Xcode (⌥⌘4). You'll see the upper and lower groups with their child objects. Clicking a group will allow you to select from the various templates in Xcode. While these templates don't allow perfect freedom in customizing the Glance, they do offer a range of different user interfaces for it. Select some templates, and then modify the labels to show some content. You may have difficulty fitting text on larger labels; to get around that, adjust the Min font scale setting in the label's Attributes Inspector to allow the text to shrink to fit. Here's an example of a Glance:

The first thing you'll want to do with a Glance is update its content. Glances are interface controllers just like the InterfaceController you modified earlier, so now you need to create a new one for the Glance. Select File → New → File… in Xcode and choose WatchKit Class from the watchOS templates. Name it GlanceInterfaceController and make it a subclass of WKInterfaceController. Make sure the language is set to Swift to match the rest of the project, and click Next. Save it in the HelloWatch WatchKit Extension folder and ensure that the WatchKit extension is the only target checked at the bottom of the dialog. Click Create, and your new class is available. You don't need to write any code in it; instead, head back to Interface.storyboard and select the Glance interface controller you created. Open the Identity Inspector (⌥⌘3) and enter GlanceInterfaceController for the Class value. Now WatchKit knows what class to create for your Glance. To update content, it's just the same as our HelloWatch example: set @IBOutlet connections for the UI elements and update their contents.

How do you test your Glance? The easiest way is to set up a new scheme in Xcode to launch the Glance. Select Product → Scheme → Manage Schemes in Xcode and a scheme dialog will appear. You should see HelloWatch and HelloWatch WatchKit App as schemes. Click the WatchKit App scheme; then click the gear icon at the bottom of the dialog and select Duplicate. In the next dialog, change the name from Copy Of HelloWatch WatchKit App to HelloWatch WatchKit App - Glance. Select Run from the left column and open the Info tab. Change the value next to Watch Interface from Main to Glance. This will run the Glance when you run this scheme from Xcode. Try it now; you should see your labels from the storyboard. If you click the Glance's UI, the main WatchKit app will open.

Glances are a nice way to provide some quick information to your users. Used properly, they can integrate your app into your users' daily routine and really become a part of their life. You'll see more on Glances later in the book and learn how powerful they can be. Now that you've seen some more of how WatchKit extensions are organized, you might be wondering why HelloWatch has three parts: an iOS app, a WatchKit app, and a WatchKit extension. Let's look at the relationship among the three.

The iPhone App–WatchKit Extension Relationship

I know what you're thinking. That *was* a lot of setup for a little "Hello, World!" app. Why so complicated? The reason lies in that WatchKit extension you created. It's a lot like other extensions on iOS—sharing, activity, photo editing, and the like—in that it's basically a tiny app that lives *inside* your main iPhone app. Unlike the other app extensions, the WatchKit app doesn't run on your phone. In fact, it's not even compiled against the iOS SDK. Instead, it's copied to the watch when you install the watch app, and it's run on the watch. Instead of iOS, it's built for watchOS. The WatchKit extension is responsible for all communication between your phone and the watch, but it doesn't manage the user interface of the app at all. Instead, it communicates with the other folder group in the template: the *WatchKit App*.

The WatchKit App's folder is pretty sparse at this point: your Interface.storyboard file, some placeholders for image assets, and an Info.plist. No code in sight. Crucially, however, *all* of the watch app's UI will reside in the WatchKit App portion of the project. Instead of creating UI objects in code, you'll put them in your storyboard, and your code will instruct the watch app on how to use them. This setup is a pretty severe departure from the way things work in iOS and is the model–view–controller paradigm taken to the extreme: your model and controller classes are separated entirely from your views.

> ∖⁄⁄ **Joe asks:**
> ˘˘ # Why Is the WatchKit App Separate?
>
> If this is your first experience writing apps for the Apple Watch, this separation of app code and user interface resources may seem arbitrary or unintuitive. Why did Apple decide to partition the apps this way? We can trace it back to how WatchKit extensions and WatchKit apps worked on the first version of WatchKit, before iOS 9 and watchOS 2. Instead of the WatchKit extension being compiled for watchOS, as we have today, WatchKit extensions were compiled as regular app extensions in iOS. Instead of being copied to the watch and executing on its processor, WatchKit extensions were left on the phone, were run on the phone, and communicated user interface changes over Bluetooth to the watch. This had a significant performance impact on the apps, but had an advantage in battery life for the watch—the heavy lifting of computation for the app was handled entirely on the phone.

WatchKit is the brains of this operation. The interface objects you use in your WatchKit extension are not the same as the objects drawn in the WatchKit app; they're representations thereof and have some nifty behaviors. To conserve power, multiple updates to your UI are coalesced into one. If you update the text of a label 15 times in one method call, that's fine; only the last value will appear on the label (though that would still be a code smell). You can think of interface objects in the WatchKit extension as proxies to their WatchKit app counterparts, even though they're on the same device. In the end, the iOS app, WatchKit app, and WatchKit extension are packaged into one bundle in the iOS App Store, making the installation process for users simple. Before you ship to the App Store, you'll probably want to test your app on a real Apple Watch, and for that, you'll need to do some code signing.

Deployment of WatchKit Apps

The iOS Simulator is a fantastic piece of software—just ask anyone who's ever tried to use an Android emulator. It is, however, a *simulator*, not an *emulator*, so you'll want to test your app on a real watch sooner rather than later. Just as you'd do for any other iOS app, you'll need to properly code-sign your app to deploy it to the watch. Code signing is the bane of many iOS developers' existence, even experienced ones, so don't worry if it doesn't work for you on your first try—or tenth. Let's look at the code-signing process as it relates to getting an Apple Watch app to run on a real Apple Watch.

Before it can run on any device, an app needs to have a valid *provisioning profile*. In short, the provisioning profile defines three things: *which app* the profile is for, *who* is allowed to digitally sign the app with a private key and certificate, and *on which devices* the final product can run. WatchKit adds a fair amount of complexity to the process. Your WatchKit extension *and* your WatchKit app must be code-signed. Luckily, if you set up everything through Xcode and are using an individual developer account rather than a large team or enterprise account, it should "just work," though there are some gotchas.

Navigate to the project settings in Xcode and look at the General tab for WatchKit Extension Target; you'll see that the bundle identifier has the suffix .watchkitapp.watchkitextension. If your provisioning profile is not a wildcard profile, it won't be able to sign that, so you'll need to create a separate app ID in the developer portal and issue a new provisioning profile and then repeat the process for the WatchKit app target. (If you've never created a provisioning profile or done code signing for an iOS app, it may be helpful to read the Code Signing documentation.[1]) If you've created any other app extensions, you'll be familiar with this process. Make sure that any devices you want to use are on all of the provisioning profiles in your app. If that sounds like a headache, it may be best to use a wildcard until you're ready to submit.

When you're all set with your app and ready to submit to the App Store, you'll go about it the exact same way. Whether you're making separate provisioning profiles or using a wildcard, your distribution profile is used to sign everything, package it up, and send it to the store. You can expect a more thorough review than you may have experienced before, since Apple will have to review both your iPhone app and your watch app. There's no separate submission for WatchKit apps—they are, after all, simply packaged into your iPhone app—so a rejection of one means a rejection of the other. You'll definitely want to test the heck out of your apps and be ready to respond to rejections quickly.

Wrap-Up

You now have an iPhone app with a WatchKit extension to play around with in the iOS Simulator and on Apple Watch if you have one. You also have a better understanding of how WatchKit extensions and WatchKit apps go hand in hand to extend your iPhone apps. Go ahead and play around a little with the objects in the Object Library in your storyboard. Look at the options available to customize the interface objects in Xcode's Attributes Inspector. In the next chapter we'll take an in-depth look at the various interface objects in WatchKit and get one step closer to writing our killer app.

---

1. https://developer.apple.com/support/code-signing

WatchKit User Interfaces

Our HelloWatch example from the prior chapter worked, but it's not winning an Apple Design Award anytime soon. We need more than just a button and a label in our WatchKit apps. We're in luck, because WatchKit offers a bevy of built-in user interface components. These UI components, called *interface objects* in WatchKit, inherit from the WKInterfaceObject class, similar to UIView in iOS. WatchKit has a unique layout system more akin to HTML tables than iOS views. Let's take a quick tour of interface objects and how they're used; then we'll explore how they differ from UIView and its subclasses. By the end of this chapter, you'll have a better understanding of what UI components are available to you in WatchKit, as well as how to position them onscreen in WatchKit's UI paradigm. Finally, you'll get started on *TapALap*, the main sample app we'll be writing throughout the rest of this book.

Meet WKInterfaceObject

When you're making user interfaces for 38mm and 42mm screen sizes, every user interface element on the screen must be carefully considered. Not only can fewer elements fit on the screen than on iOS, but due to the smaller size, the user's finger will necessarily obscure more of the screen while interacting with it. These truths impact the design of every element, as well as the overall design of watchOS apps in general.

From a code standpoint, there's a huge difference between UIView and WKInterfaceObject: you cannot subclass WKInterfaceObject to create your own user interface objects. Instead of implementing custom rendering and touch handling, watchOS apps compose the built-in interface objects and achieve their desired user interface customizations through images and colors. You'll also notice that instead of setting properties on the interface objects directly, you'll be calling methods on the objects to set their properties indirectly. The reason for this indirection is that the interface objects aren't *really* in the WatchKit extension that we're writing. As you learned on page 12, the WatchKit app and WatchKit extension are separate entities on the device, and the interface objects live in the WatchKit app portion. The WKInterfaceObject instances we deal with in the WatchKit extension represent the objects onscreen. Why methods instead of properties? They're write-only; you can't inspect an interface object for its state. Because neither Swift nor Objective-C has a mechanism for write-only properties, this changes a simple task, such as setting the text of a label. Where you would write this for iOS

```
self.label.text = "Hello, World!"
```

the equivalent code for a watchOS application would look like this:

```
self.label.setText("Hello, World!")
```

All WKInterfaceObject objects share some common properties that you can set, either by calling methods on them or directly in the storyboard. Most of them are familiar, if slightly different than their UIView counterparts: you can set their width, height, and alpha, as well as make them hidden. In the storyboard, you can check the Installed check box to determine if an interface object is created when the storyboard loads. From there, the individual interface object classes define more properties that you can set. Instead of enumerating them one-by-one, we'll look at them in three categories: objects that display data, objects that receive user input, and objects used for layout.

Objects that Display Data

You've already seen one of these interface objects, WKInterfaceLabel, which you used to display "Hello, Watch!" to your users. Labels act much like UILabel in UIKit, and you can call setText() or setAttributedText() to change their contents, just like in UIKit. The other objects in this category include WKInterfaceTimer and WKInterfaceDate, which help your watch app tell time. A timer object counts down to a given moment in time, represented by an NSDate, using a format you specify. The format must be specified in Interface Builder, but once you've created your timer, you can change it by calling setDate() on it. Using its start() and stop() methods, you can control whether your WKInterfaceTimer updates, though it always counts down to the same date, regardless of you stopping it. Finally, WKInterfaceDate displays the current date and/or time to the user in a label. Like setting up a timer, you must set up your date formatting in Interface Builder. Once you've created a date object, you can use setTimeZone() and setCalendar() to adjust the display of the date. There are three more interface objects in this category, and you can see them all in this image.

Interface objects for displaying data to the user. From top to bottom: WKInterfaceLabel, WKInterfaceDate, WKInterfaceTimer, WKInterfaceImage, WKInterfaceMovie, and
WKInterfaceMap.

Another important object is WKInterfaceImage, which acts like UIImageView on iOS,
displaying images to the user. Image objects support displaying static and
animated images with setImage(_:), setImageData(_:), and setImageNamed(_:) methods,
and if you supply template images, you can provide a tint color using setTint-
Color(_:). Images in your WatchKit app can come from your watch app's asset
catalog or your WatchKit extension.

WKInterfaceMovie is a similar class to WKInterfaceImage but for movies instead of images. You can set a placeholder image using setPosterImage(_:) and a movie URL using setMovieURL(_:). When the user taps the Play button, the movie will begin playback if it's stored locally on the device; otherwise, it'll download before playing. WKInterfaceMovie doesn't support streaming, so if you want to watch Netflix and chill, you won't be doing it on your wrist. In general, the watch is not designed to play movies, but for short clips, it can do in a pinch.

The last interface object you can use to display data to the user is WKInterfaceMap. Like its MKMapView counterpart, the map object displays a map using Apple's mapping service. You can add your own pins to the map using its addAnnotation(_:withPinColor:) method, allowing you to show locations to your users. If you have a custom image to use instead of the default colored pins, you can use addAnnotation(_:withImage:centerOffset:) or addAnnotation(_:withImageNamed:centerOffset:), providing an offset in case you need to move the pin image relative to the map location (normally the pin image is centered over the location). You'll want to position the map in the proper location so users see your pins, which you'll do with setVisibleMapRect() or setRegion(). These methods take the same MapKit types as MKMapView.

Interacting with Maps

There's one caveat to using WKInterfaceMap: once you position the map, users can't interact with it. There's no zooming, panning, or selecting of pins. Scrolling the watch's Digital Crown will only scroll your interface controller's content, if there's enough to scroll. When the user taps the map, the watch's Maps app opens. The center of the visible location of your map is a pin in the user's Maps app. This allows your users to get directions or anything else they'd be able to do in the Maps app normally. If you want to display a specific location to users, set that location as the center of your map; in the Maps app on the watch, the users will be able to get directions or anything else they'd normally do with a map location.

Objects that Receive User Input

On iOS, user interface objects that respond to user input derive from the UIControl class, itself a subclass of UIView. Although there's no equivalent intermediate class in WatchKit, some interface objects embody the spirit behind controls on iOS. You've already seen WKInterfaceButton, which allows you to call a method when the user taps the button. Unlike UIControl's action methods that you can add with addTarget(_:action:forControlEvents:), you have to connect

WKInterfaceButton objects to @IBAction methods in your storyboard. Aside from buttons, there are switches and sliders: WKInterfaceSwitch and WKInterfaceSlider, respectively. They mostly act like UISwitch and UISlider, with a few differences. Visually, a WKInterfaceSwitch looks a lot like a WKInterfaceButton, with a title label in front of the background, but there's also a switch control on the right side. Sliders have a similar appearance, with incrementing and decrementing buttons on either side and the main slider in the middle. You can see all of these objects in this image.

Interface objects for receiving input from your user. From top to bottom: WKInterfaceButton, WKInterfaceSwitch, WKInterfaceSlider, and WKInterfacePicker.

Sliders and switches, just like buttons, require you to set up the method they call in your storyboard. The method you write for a switch must take a Bool parameter for the switch's value, and a slider's method must take a Float. Both are called every time the user adjusts the value. For sliders you have some additional control: in the storyboard you can set the minimum and maximum value for the slider, and either in the storyboard or by calling setNumberOfSteps() you can set the number of steps between those values. If you wanted to make a slider that could select any integral value between 0 and 5, you'd set the minimum to 0, the maximum to 5, and the number of steps to 6.

New in watchOS 2 is a fantastic interface object for getting user input: WKInterfacePicker. A picker allows the user to select from a list of elements. These elements can be text, images, or both. What's unique about pickers is that instead of swiping the screen, as they might on iOS, your users will use the Digital Crown on the side of the Apple Watch to select the values. This interaction feels great, whether selecting from photos in a photo album, remotely controlling the climate settings in their car, or fine-tuning a setting with more precision than a slider would comfortably allow. You can even place multiple pickers onscreen at once; the currently active picker is optionally highlighted with a green border and optional caption, as shown here:

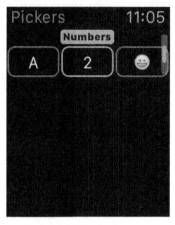

Three WKInterfacePicker objects in one interface controller; the middle one is selected with the caption Numbers.

You'll see more on pickers in depth later on page 78 as you add one to your sample app. Pickers allow you to replace complicated input schemes like text entry with simple Digital Crown interactions, so they're a great addition to any app that needs any input from a user.

Objects Used for Layout

The final category of interface objects is an interesting one; these objects exist to help out with WatchKit's unique layout system. The most important of these is WKInterfaceGroup, which is so vital to the watch UI that it has its own chapter coming up. In short, a group can contain other objects, allowing you more freedom in how they're laid out. Groups can even contain other groups, allowing you to create complex hierarchies of layout. Along with groups comes WKInterfaceSeparator, which is by far the simplest of all interface objects—it's basically a line drawn between other objects to separate them, and it has but one method for you to call, setColor().

The final interface object that helps with layout is WKInterfaceTable. Since every interface object you use must be created in your storyboard, using a table is one of the only ways to get dynamic content into your app. Each row in the table is actually a group, so you can lay out whatever objects you need in each row. (More on tables later, in their own chapter.)

Creating Interface Objects

Remember in the last chapter, on page 9, when you dragged your first interface object onto the blank canvas of your storyboard? That black area inside the Interface Builder canvas was your *interface controller*. Think of an interface controller like a view controller, its iOS equivalent; they both manage screenfuls of content—albeit a much smaller screen on the watch. When your WatchKit app loads, whichever interface controller in the storyboard is set to be the initial controller, signified by an arrow pointing to it, will display first. There are two ways to change which interface controller gets loaded first: dragging the arrow around in your storyboard or selecting the interface controller, navigating to Xcode's Attributes Inspector (⌥⌘4), and checking the Is Initial Controller check box.

Every interface controller needs an associated class, and that class needs to be a subclass of WKInterfaceController. In our HelloWatch example, Xcode created an interface controller class named InterfaceController. Creative, right? Now you may be wondering how you create your own interface controllers. For iOS you have two options: in the storyboard or in code. Once you have a UIViewController subclass, it's easy to do either way. WKInterfaceControllers in WatchKit, on the other hand, can't be created in code; you can *only* create them in your WatchKit app's storyboard.

In the last chapter when I mentioned that you would be creating all of your watch UI in your storyboard, I wasn't just telling you best practices or leading you down the easiest path; you literally cannot create any interface objects—including interface controllers—in code. If you try to call InterfaceController() to create a new interface controller in HelloWatch, your app will crash. Similarly, if you try to create a new interface object to put in your interface controller by calling, say, WKInterfaceLabel(), the returned object will be nil! Because you can't create interface objects programmatically, your storyboard must contain everything your app needs.

Designing Your UI in the Storyboard

With every interface object created in your storyboard, how can you hope to make the UI you want? Great watch user interfaces will separate themselves from the built-in UI. Much like iOS apps use custom interfaces to establish their brand, you can apply a few techniques to make your designs great while still creating nearly everything in your storyboard.

Hiding Inactive Objects

One clever trick for a great UI is using the setHidden() method of WKInterfaceObject. If you mark an interface object as hidden, it's removed from the screen and from the layout system, so everything else will move around accordingly. If you have two mutually exclusive states you want to display, make them *both* and then hide the one you don't need. When you want to switch states, call setHidden() on them both with opposite values. Creating two duplicate interfaces may seem wasteful, but it allows you to be explicit with your UI's options. Several of the properties of interface objects can't be set once they're created in the storyboard, so don't feel bad about creating both states.

Joe asks:

How Do I Know Which Properties I Can Set in Code?

For every WKInterfaceObject subclass, as well as WKInterfaceController, Apple's documentation includes a section in its introduction called Interface Builder Configuration Options. The documentation also displays the methods to call to change attributes; if there's no method listed for a particular attribute, then you can change it only in the story-board. For instance, you can set the background *image* of a WKInterfaceButton using setBackgroundImage(), but you can change the background *color* only in the storyboard.

Using Images Effectively

Another trick to making a great UI is to take advantage of images. Not only can you place images directly in your layout with WKInterfaceImage, but other classes support background images that appear behind other interface objects. WKInterfaceGroup allows you to set a background image in code or in your story-board. Since groups contain other interface objects, this allows you to create an image that sits behind other objects. WKInterfaceController and WKInterfaceTable also support background images but only at design time in your storyboard. Using background images is a great way to add some flavor to your app and give everything a cohesive design.

Images in the foreground don't have to be large photographs. Using small, iconographic images draws your user's attention to your content. A button with text is descriptive, but a button with text next to an icon conveys more information. Now, to be honest, I'm not a designer. If you aren't either, you'll want to consult one for better image advice. Shipping an app with programmer art may work, but a professional designer can take your app to another level.

Using Color and Type

Another factor in making great-looking watch apps is effective use of color and type. While most interface controllers should have black backgrounds, per convention,[1] a splash of color can go a long way. You can define a main tint color for your app in your storyboard by opening the File Inspector (⌥⌘1) and changing the value for Global Tint, which affects the color of UI elements such as the title bar at the top of the screen.

While it's possible to use custom fonts in your WatchKit app the same way you can in iOS, think long and hard about it. Because Apple Watch allows the user to select the font size (a feature called Dynamic Type), built-in interface objects using the system font automatically use different font sizes when necessary. If you want to use your own font, you'll need to implement this yourself, adjusting the size of fonts you use based on the user's selection. Keep in mind that if you use a Glance you can't use custom fonts, since your app isn't loaded.

There's one huge part of WatchKit interfaces that we haven't covered yet, though you may have already encountered it in Interface Builder: you can't move things around! If you try to drag an interface object in its interface controller, it snaps into place. This layout system takes some getting used to, but it can be very powerful once you understand it.

Interface Object Layout

By far the most striking difference between WatchKit and UIKit user interface development is their different approaches to layout. On iOS you have free control over the placement of views. You can overlap them, rotate them, and place them anywhere onscreen. WatchKit, as you may have noticed, places everything for you. Try it out: go to your storyboard, make a new interface controller, and drag in a few buttons or labels. You'll notice that they appear in order, one below the next; the system places them on the screen in the order in which they appear in the Document Outline. If you add tons of interface objects, you'll notice that interface controllers automatically scroll their contents when necessary; this is accomplished by swiping or by rotating the Digital Crown (on a real device only).

Order matters in WatchKit's UI system. The storyboard's Document Outline, accessible by selecting Editor → Show Document Outline, reveals the order

---

1. See the Apple Watch Human Interface Guidelines at developer.apple.com/library/ios/documentation/UserExperience/Conceptual/WatchHumanInterfaceGuidelines/index.html for more information on using color in your app.

of your objects and allows you to reorder them by dragging. Aside from this order, there are some Interface Builder settings you can use to force the layout to do your bidding. By setting the Vertical and Horizontal values under Position in the Attributes Inspector, you can make an object left-, center-, or right-aligned horizontally and top-, center-, or bottom-aligned vertically. In the following screenshot, labels A, B, C, and D are in order alphabetically, but since label C is configured to be at the bottom vertically, it's moved below label D.

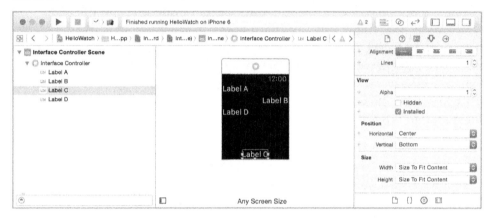

These controls over alignment are indispensable for getting your layout to where you want it. You can also adjust the size of interface objects. Most of them default to Size To Fit Content, but you can override that with either a fixed size in points or a size relative to the object's container. Setting an object's height relative to its container to 0.5, for instance, will cause it to fill up half of the container vertically.

For a better handle on custom layouts, it's time to get your feet wet with WatchKit. Let's start creating TapALap, the sample app that you will work on in this book.

Creating Your Apple Watch App

While going for a run, you want to know things like how far you've traveled and how fast you're moving. Plenty of apps exist to do this *outside*, where your iPhone gets great GPS reception, but you want one that works great *indoors* on a track. That is the purpose of the Apple Watch app we'll be creating together in this book. You'll be building a rudimentary stopwatch; every time users cross the starting line of the lap, they'll tap a button to mark a lap as completed, and the app will mark the time they tapped the button. Inspired by this user interface, the app is named *TapALap*, since you're *tapping* a *lap*.

I know—*amazing* name. Every track is a different size; the one at my local gym, for instance, is five laps to a mile. So your app will need a screen to start and stop a run as well as mark a lap as complete, and another screen to specify how long your track is.

Creating the Xcode Project

To get started, open Xcode and select File → New → Project. Select the iOS App with WatchKit App template under the watchOS section. On the next screen, enter TapALap as the product name. I'll use Pragmatic Bookshelf and com.pragprog as the organization name and identifier, but use whatever you'd like. We'll use Swift for the language. Underneath the language selection, uncheck all of the optional check boxes. Finally, make sure iPhone is the selected device. Choose Next, find a place to save the app, and choose Create.

Joe asks:
Why Aren't We Including Tests?

You may have noticed two check boxes that we disabled when we created the TapALap project: Include Unit Tests and Include UI Tests. Those sound like good things to have, so why not enable them?

Fact is, WatchKit is still a very young platform, and the tools in Xcode don't really support tests yet. You can't run UI tests on your WatchKit app—they're limited to iOS and OS X apps for now—and your unit tests can't target your WatchKit extension. If you want to have tested code in your WatchKit app, you'll need to extract it into a framework for which you can run unit tests. It's definitely not an ideal situation, so hopefully future versions of Xcode will be able to do more watchOS testing.

The first thing you need in this app is a screen to start the run. This will be the app's main task, so you want that screen to be the first thing users see when they open it. By default, Xcode created an interface controller class called, appropriately enough, InterfaceController.

Renaming the Interface Controller

You'll have numerous interface controllers by the time this is done, so before we continue, let's rename this class. To give InterfaceController a better name, select InterfaceController.swift in Xcode's Project Navigator (it should be in the TapALap WatchKit Extension group) and then press ↵ to rename it as GoRunningInterfaceController.swift.

Once the file is renamed, you need to rename the class. Open GoRunningInterfaceController.swift and rename the class so its declaration looks like this:

```
class GoRunningInterfaceController: WKInterfaceController {

}
```

Next, you need to rename it in the storyboard. Open Interface.storyboard and select the interface controller. In the Identity Inspector (⌘⌥3), change the Class value to GoRunningInterfaceController. Now the three-step renaming process is complete! This tedious process is a sign of Swift's relative immaturity compared to other languages; once the Xcode tools around it mature, renaming classes and other refactoring tasks should get a *lot* easier.

Creating Your Interface

It's time to start adding UI elements. The most important is a button to start running—after all, isn't that the point of the app? Open the Interface.storyboard file again and select the interface controller. To better identify it later when you have others, select and title it "Go Running" in the Attributes Inspector. Next, open Xcode's Object Library (^⌥⌘3) and drag a new WKInterfaceButton (named *Button* in the library's list) onto the interface controller. This will be your Start Run button, title it "Start Run" in the Attributes Inspector and set its background color to green. This button is set for now—you'll hook up this button to some code later on page 64. This interface controller is also complete for now—in the next chapter on page 33, you'll add a more complex UI to it.

Aside from a screen to start running, you need a screen to display when the user is on a run. In your storyboard, open Xcode's Object Library again and drag out a new interface controller. Use the Attributes Inspector to set its title to "Run." Add a new button to it with a red background; this will be the Stop Run button, so set that as its title. You also want a button to mark a lap as finished, so drag in a new button and give it the title "Finish Lap." Finally, your users will want to know how far they've run, so add two more labels to the controller. Set the first one's text style to Headline and its title to "Total Distance:" (with the colon). Set the second label's text style to "Subhead." Since you'll set its value in code, leave its text alone for now.

Create a new WKInterfaceController subclass for this interface controller, named RunTimerInterfaceController. Select the interface controller in the storyboard and change its class in the Identity Inspector (⌥⌘3) to RunTimerInterfaceController. It is time to hook up some code to the buttons. Open Xcode's Assistant Editor (⌥⌘↵) and select the interface controller in your storyboard. If the interface-controller class doesn't appear in the Assistant Editor, reset it with ⌥⇧⌘Z.

Connecting UI and Code

When you're finished with this project, the Stop Run button will finish the run and transition to a different screen, but for now let's just hook it up to the code. Control-drag from the button to your interface controller's code—between the curly braces—and select Action from the Connection drop-down, naming it stopRunButtonPressed(). You'll have that method call endRun(), another method you'll create in your interface controller and in which you'll be implementing a lot of this app's logic:

Chapter 3/TapALap/TapALap WatchKit Extension/RunTimerInterfaceController.swift

```
@IBAction func stopRunButtonPressed() {
    endRun()
}

func endRun() {

}
```

Next, you want a way to update your Total Distance label. To do that, you need a way to reference the label from code. Control-drag from the second label to the top of the class. Choose Outlet from the Connection drop-down and name it distanceLabel. You don't need an outlet for the first label; its text doesn't change. Now you can update the label's text using its setText() method. But how do you know how far one lap is? You need some data in your object—a Track struct would be prudent. You don't need to do much more than store data in it, so using a struct instead of a class helps cut down on the code you need to write.

Creating Data Structures

In Xcode, select File → New → File, and choose the Swift File template. Name the file Track.swift. Ensure that the file is added to the TapALap WatchKit Extension target, and then create it. Once you've created the file, implementing the struct is short—it only needs to store a name and a lap distance:

Chapter 3/TapALap/TapALap WatchKit Extension/Track.swift

```
struct Track {
    let name: String
    let lapDistance: Double // in meters
}
```

Later you'll allow users to configure their own tracks. For now you'll create a temporary Track instance for use in your calculations. Head back to RunTimer-InterfaceController.swift and add a new property to store the Track. You'll make it lazy so that it'll be created as needed:

Chapter 3/TapALap/TapALap WatchKit Extension/RunTimerInterfaceController.swift

```
lazy var track: Track = Track(name: "Track", lapDistance:  500)
```

This creates a track named Track, with a distance per lap of 500 meters. When the user taps the Finish Lap button, you'll add 500 meters to the total distance, marking the time at which the lap is finished. All you really need to store is how long each lap was in terms of time, since you know the distance is the same for each lap. You can simply add an array of NSTimeInterval values for each lap:

Chapter 3/TapALap/TapALap WatchKit Extension/RunTimerInterfaceController.swift

```
var lapTimes: [NSTimeInterval]?
var startDate: NSDate?
```

 Joe asks:
When Is willActivate Called?

Interface controllers, much like their view controller counterparts, have a set of *life-cycle* methods that your subclasses can implement to customize their functionality. There are far fewer for WKInterfaceController, but the important ones are there. Here they are, in order:

1. init()—Called when an interface controller instance is created. Use it to perform any one-time setup you need to do.

2. awakeWithContext()—Called when an interface controller is initialized, optionally with contextual information provided.

3. willActivate()—Called immediately before the interface controller appears on the screen. Use this method to ensure that the data presented by the interface controller is up to date.

4. didDeactivate()—Called when the interface controller disappears. Use this method to clean up any resources used by the interface controller.

You don't need to implement each of these lifecycle methods in each interface-controller class you make, but it's a good idea to be familiar with them and to know which tasks belong in which method.

You'll want to initialize this array at the beginning of the user's run, which is right when this interface controller appears onscreen. To do that, implement the interface controller's willActivate() method. You'll want to do this only if the array is currently nil; if the user leaves your app and comes back to it, willActivate() will be called again, and you'll want to preserve the user's current run. Add the method now:

```
override func willActivate() {
    super.willActivate()

    if lapTimes == nil || startDate == nil {
        lapTimes = []
        startDate = NSDate()
    }
}
```

Every time a user finishes a lap, you want to add the lap's duration to the lapTimes array and update the total distance label. To prepare for this, add a new method called updateDistanceLabel(). You'll use the lapTimes array again here, multiplying its count by the track's per-lap distance. You'll create a lazy NSLengthFormatter to turn the distance into a human-readable string:

```
lazy var lengthFormatter: NSLengthFormatter = {
    let formatter = NSLengthFormatter()
    formatter.numberFormatter.maximumSignificantDigits = 3
    return formatter
}()

func updateDistanceLabel() {
    guard let lapTimes = lapTimes where !lapTimes.isEmpty else {
        distanceLabel.setText("No laps finished!")
        return
    }

    let distance = track.lapDistance * Double(lapTimes.count)

    distanceLabel.setText(lengthFormatter.stringFromMeters(distance))
}
```

Now all you need to do is to connect a new @IBAction method for the Finish Lap button in your storyboard:

```
@IBAction func finishLapButtonPressed() {
    let lapFinishTime = NSDate()

    guard let startDate = startDate, lapTimes = lapTimes else { return }

    let totalRunDuration = lapFinishTime.timeIntervalSinceDate(startDate)

    let cumulativeLapDuration = lapTimes.reduce(0, combine: { $0 + $1 })

    let lapDuration = totalRunDuration - cumulativeLapDuration

    self.lapTimes?.append(lapDuration)

    updateDistanceLabel()
}
```

When the user taps Finish Lap, the label will update. There's only one more thing left to do. Add a call to updateDistanceLabel() in the willActivate() method:

Chapter 3/TapALap/TapALap WatchKit Extension/RunTimerInterfaceController.swift

```swift
override func willActivate() {
    super.willActivate()

    if lapTimes == nil || startDate == nil {
        lapTimes = []
        startDate = NSDate()
    }

    updateDistanceLabel()
}
```

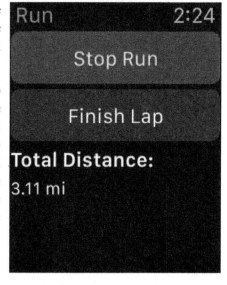

Now when you come to this screen, the distance label will be set at 0. Once the Finish Lap button is tapped, it will update automatically.

That's a good place to stop for now. To try out this interface controller, drag the Initial Controller arrow in the storyboard to it, and then run your app. As you tap Finish Lap, you will see the label update—your screen should look like the one shown here. Be sure to drag the arrow back to the Go Running interface controller when you've finished.

Wrap-Up

This chapter has given you a taste of what types of user interfaces you can make in WatchKit. You know about the main interface objects, and you've gotten some experience putting them into an app. The layouts have been fairly simple, so it's time to get a bit more advanced. The best way to exert control over layout is to use groups. You'll notice I've been using the word *container* a lot, and there's good reason. Groups allow you to define hierarchies of objects and lay them out together. They're some of the most powerful interface objects in WatchKit. We'll explore them in detail in the next chapter.

Organizing Your UI with Groups

The UI system in WatchKit is entirely linear. As you've seen thus far, when you add interface objects to an interface controller, they stack from top to bottom. Instead of using Auto Layout to position user interface objects with constraints, or the old "springs and struts" style of autoresizing masks that came before it, WatchKit handles positioning interface objects on your behalf. You probably noticed this behavior when you were adding interface objects to your storyboard.

This system of automatically positioning elements in a sequence is much more like the new UIStackView class in iOS than the other, older iOS layout paradigms. Introduced in iOS 9, UIStackView class is a container for other UIView objects. Instead of using Auto Layout constraints to position its subviews, UIStackView places them along a linear path, much like the layout system in WatchKit. Its announcement at the Apple Worldwide Developers Conference (WWDC) 2015 was met with great enthusiasm from iOS developers who had long wanted an easier approach to interface layout.

In fact, WatchKit's UI system predates UIStackView by about six months. You can adjust their relative positioning in your storyboard, but sometimes you'll want more control over your layout. That's where *groups* come in. The WKInterfaceGroup interface object acts as a container for other objects, letting you adjust the positioning and size of elements in more precise ways. You can set background colors and images for groups, hide them from your UI, animate their properties, and even nest groups together. In this chapter, you'll discover the capabilities of groups, which make interesting user interfaces possible.

Group Basics

You can think of every interface controller in your app as its own group. When you add interface objects to the interface controller, WatchKit's layout system places them in order, top to bottom. The first cool feature of groups is that you can control the direction of the layout—while the interface controller in the storyboard defaults to arranging its objects top to bottom, a group can also arrange its objects left to right. You can also specify the size of the group relative to its container, whether that's the interface controller itself or another group. And you can pick a background image or background color. Best of all, you can add a group to another group, allowing for nested groups. Nested groups allow for some extremely complicated bits of user interface, as you'll see when you build a more complicated UI later in this book. The following figure shows a quick example of nested groups.

This interface controller has two groups as children: Group A (with a green background color) and Group B. Groups A and B are set to have the full width of their container and half its height. You can see this in the Attributes Editor in the screenshot; values are in the range 0–1, so the height is set to 0.5. Group B, which is set to a horizontal group, has two children, Groups C and D. Each of those is set to the full *height* of its container and half its width, so they split it down the middle. With some labels in Groups A, C, and D, all set to center themselves horizontally and vertically, you see the result. By using groups in this example, you're able to place two elements next to one another; without Group B, Groups C and D would still appear one after another vertically, even if set to left and right, as shown here.

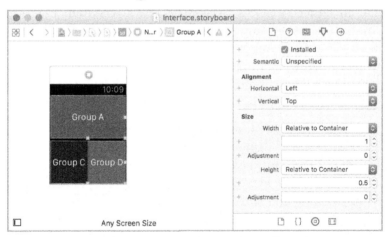

You can nest groups to your heart's content, using the relative sizes to adjust positioning. You can also set precise sizes for either width or height using points, allowing you to control the exact size of a group. These are the basics of using groups. To see more advanced features, let's head back to TapALap and make the UI more expressive.

Adding Detail to a Screen

The Go Running screen in your TapALap app is pretty bare at the moment—just a green button. There's more information you want to display on this screen: the track on which the user is about to run (with the ability to edit it) as well as some stats about the runner's overall performance. Let's do the performance stats first.

Using Groups for Advanced Layout

Your users will want to know how many runs they've been on and their average pace. To that end, let's add one group for each of those topics to the interface controller. Drag out a new group and add two labels to it. This will be the group for the number of times the user has run using your app. Change the text of the first label to a number—I use 5 in my example—so you know what it'll look like with data in it. Change the text of the second one to "Runs." It doesn't look fantastic yet, so let's make some changes to improve its appearance. Select the group and then, in the Attributes Inspector, set Layout to Vertical. Give it a dark-gray color to fill in the background, and change the Spacing property to 0. The Spacing property adjusts how close child elements are to one another, and for this example you want the labels to be relatively tight. For the size of this group, select Relative To Container for Width and enter 0.35; you can leave the height at Size To Fit Content.

Next, select the number label and increase its text size. I selected the System Bold font at 35 points. To select the font, tap the icon at the right of the font name (see the following screenshot). Set its Horizontal position to Center and its Vertical position to Top. This makes it nice and prominent in the group. For the other label, I selected the built-in Footnote text style. Change its Horizontal position to Center and its Vertical position to Bottom. For both labels, you can leave the Width and Height settings as they are.

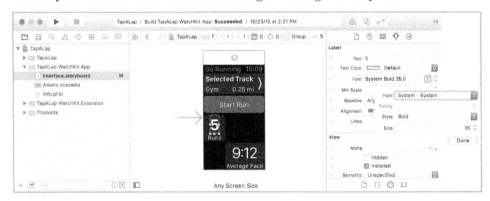

For the second group, you can select the group you just made and copy and paste it into the Document Outline. Starting with the copy of this group, you can make a few small changes. Change the width of the new group to 0.65 relative to its container and change its horizontal position to Right. Change the text of the top label to something that looks like a time; I used 9:12 even if that's a bit optimistic for my real-life running speed. Change Runs to Average Pace. I also changed the font of the pace label from Bold to Regular weight. When you've finished you'll have two groups, but they won't be next to each other (as you see here).

Select both groups, click Editor → Embed In → Horizontal Group, and they'll fit next to each other beautifully, as shown here.

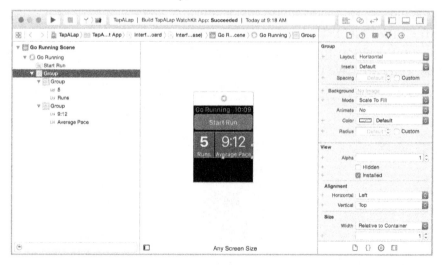

You also need a way to edit the track. For that, you'll add another WKInterface-Button, but this one will be unlike the others you've seen so far: the button *itself* will be a group.

Using Groups for Button Contents

Drag a new button onto the interface controller. You'll put this one at the top. Instead of setting a title, change the Content setting in Xcode's Attributes Inspector from Text to Group. Its appearance changes from the default button appearance to an empty group. Add three labels to the group. You'll configure them for your content next.

The first label will be a heading for this group. Change its text to "Selected Track" and its font to the built-in Headline style. This label's text won't change, so you're finished with it at this point. For the second label, change its text to "Gym" and its font to Subhead. You'll use this label for the name of the track. In case this name gets long, change its Min Scale property in the Attributes Inspector to 0.8; this allows WatchKit to shrink the text in the label by up to 20% to make things fit, maintaining a minimum font scale that you set. (The minimum font scale setting doesn't work for multiline labels; instead, they'll expand to fit their text, up to the number of lines you specify. If you specify 0 lines, the label will automatically use as many lines as it takes to fit its content.) The third label will show how long each lap of the track is. Change its text to "0.25 mi" and its font to Caption 2. Change its minimum scale to 0.75.

The button is looking OK, but it could look better. Let's start with the label positioning. First, change the group inside the button's layout to Vertical. Change the lap distance label's Horizontal position to Right, and then embed it and the track name label in a horizontal group. This places them side by side and frees up some screen space. Next, you want to bring the contents in a little; by default, they extend to the edge a bit too much for my taste. Select the group directly underneath the button in the Document Outline, open Xcode's Attributes Inspector, and change its Insets value to Custom. When you do, you'll notice four new values to set. Change the Top and Bottom insets to 2 and the Left and Right insets to 4. This will bring in your content nicely. Next, set the Color property of the group to the same dark-gray color you used for the statistics groups.

Build and run the app. Notice that you can tap the Start Run button, and it will compress when you tap it, but you can *also* tap the Selected Track button, and it will compress with all of its contents. This may be confusing to users, because the top button looks similar to the lower groups, so let's make one final change. Similar to the disclosure indicator for a table-view cell on iOS, you'll use a right-facing chevron to indicate that tapping the button will go to a different interface controller. I've created a simple chevron image that you can find in the book's source code.[1] In the Project Navigator, open the Assets.xcassets asset collection in the TapALap WatchKit App group. Add chevron@2x.png as a new image asset named chevron. Head back to the button group and add a new WKInterfaceImage (named *Image* in the library) to it. In the Attributes Inspector, change its Image property to chevron, and you'll see the image you added. It will be there but in the wrong place entirely.

To fix the positioning of this image, you need more groups. Ideally the chevron image will be at the right side of the button, centered vertically. To begin, set its horizontal position to Right and its vertical position to Center. Now, you want to put this in a horizontal group with your other content, but you want the existing content to remain vertically oriented. Select the Selected Track label and the group containing the other labels, and embed them in their own vertical group. This won't fix the problem, but it will let you perform the next step: change the group directly underneath the button's layout back to Horizontal. The image disappears! It's actually still there but pushed offscreen. Select the vertical group you made for the three labels and change its Width property to Relative To Container. To bring in the right side and display the image, set the Adjustment property to −12. Now you can see all of the labels as well as the chevron image. If your interface controller looks like the image here, you've done everything correctly.

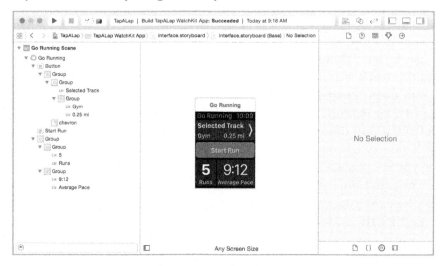

---

1. You can find the source code at https://pragprog.com/titles/jkwatch2/source_code/. The image is at the path TapALap/TapALap WatchKit App/Assets.xcassets/chevron.imageset/.

As you can see, groups give you fine-grained control over your app's contents. Apps aren't design comps, however; they move around, respond to their users, and update accordingly. So next let's see how groups can help you with amazing animations.

Animation and Groups

As you saw earlier, WKInterfaceController's animateWithDuration(duration:animations:) method allows you to update properties of your interface objects inside an animation. WKInterfaceGroup is no different, and you can animate all sorts of properties, just like other interface objects. One animation property belongs to groups alone, and that is the *content inset*. This inset allows you to push content back from the edge of the group, and it can be useful for moving an object around the screen with more control than simple horizontal or vertical alignment.

To illustrate group animations, let's make a simple watchOS game. Turns out, we can make one to illustrate group animation in about 100 lines of Swift! Our simple "game" will have a white ball on a green field and buttons to virtually "kick" the ball around on the screen. It's not much, but my three-year-old loves it! In Xcode, select File → New → Project..., and then select iOS App with WatchKit App from the Watch OS section. Name it "Soccer"—or "Football" if you're outside the United States—and click Next. Then save it. In the project that opens, head to the watch app target's Interface.storyboard storyboard, and add two groups. You'll use the top one for the field, so select it, and then in Xcode's Attributes Inspector, give it a green background. You want it to mostly fill the screen, so change its width and height to Relative to Container with a value of 1. To give you room for some buttons below, give it a Height Adjustment of -44. Next, you'll add the ball as another group inside the soccer field group. Give this one a white background. To make it round, give it a fixed width and height of 20 and a corner radius of 10. It'll look like a circle, exactly what you want!

In the bottom group, add two buttons. One will move the ball horizontally and the other vertically. Set their widths to 50% relative to their container, and set their heights to 44 to match the offset of the field. For the left one, which will move the ball vertically, set its title to ↓ (if you're having trouble with that character, select Edit → Emoji & Symbols to bring up an entry pane and navigate to the Bullets/Stars section). The right button will control the horizontal position of the ball, so set its title to →. The interface controller should look as shown in the figure on page 38.

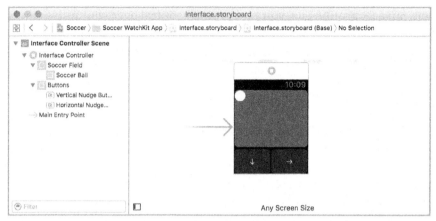

Let's head to the code. Open the InterfaceController.swift file that the Xcode template helpfully created. You can remove the existing methods, because you won't be using them. To begin, you'll add @IBOutlets for your interface objects:

Chapter 4/Soccer/Soccer WatchKit Extension/InterfaceController.swift

```
@IBOutlet weak var soccerBall: WKInterfaceGroup!
@IBOutlet weak var soccerField: WKInterfaceGroup!
@IBOutlet weak var verticalNudgeButton: WKInterfaceButton!
@IBOutlet weak var horizontalNudgeButton: WKInterfaceButton!
```

Head back to Interface.storyboard and connect the interface controller to these outlets by Control-dragging from the interface controller to the elements. Once they're all connected to the appropriate objects, open InterfaceController.swift and add a new type to represent the direction the ball is moving:

Chapter 4/Soccer/Soccer WatchKit Extension/InterfaceController.swift

```
enum ButtonDirection: String {
    case Up = "↑"
    case Down = "↓"
    case Left = "←"
    case Right = "→"
}
```

The raw value of this enumeration type is String, you'll use its values to populate buttons as they change. To do this, you'll store the vertical and horizontal direction as properties, then update the buttons' titles when they change:

Chapter 4/Soccer/Soccer WatchKit Extension/InterfaceController.swift

```
var verticalDirection: ButtonDirection = .Down {
    didSet {
        verticalNudgeButton.setTitle(verticalDirection.rawValue)
    }
}
```

```
var horizontalDirection: ButtonDirection = .Right {
    didSet {
        horizontalNudgeButton.setTitle(horizontalDirection.rawValue)
    }
}
```

In both cases, you use the didSet() property observer to set the appropriate button's title using the enum's rawValue property.

Next, some other properties to help keep track of the game's current state:

Chapter 4/Soccer/Soccer WatchKit Extension/InterfaceController.swift

```
let ballSize: CGSize = CGSize(width: 20, height: 20)
var currentInsets: UIEdgeInsets = UIEdgeInsetsZero

var soccerFieldSize: CGSize {
    var frame = contentFrame
    frame.size.height -= 44
    return frame.size
}
```

The ballSize constant allows you to compute the ball's position, along with the currentInsets property. The insets start as UIEdgeInsetsZero, since the ball starts in the upper-left corner. Finally, you have the soccerFieldSize, which lets you know the size (in points) of the soccer field, so you don't let the ball leave its field. To get that size, all you need to do is subtract the 44 points you left for the buttons from the interface controller's contentFrame property.

In this method, you can use the contentFrame property of the interface controller to derive the soccer field size, which is equal but for the 44 points on the bottom where the buttons sit. With that in place, you just need to animate the ball when a user presses a button:

Chapter 4/Soccer/Soccer WatchKit Extension/InterfaceController.swift

```
let kickDistance: CGFloat = 10
let kickDuration = 1.0 / 3.0

@IBAction func verticalNudgeButtonPressed() {
    if verticalDirection == .Down {
        currentInsets.top += kickDistance

        if currentInsets.top + ballSize.height + kickDistance >
            soccerFieldSize.height {
                verticalDirection = .Up
        }
    }
    else {
        currentInsets.top -= kickDistance

        if currentInsets.top - kickDistance < 0 {
```

```
                verticalDirection = .Down
            }
        }

    animateWithDuration(kickDuration) {
        self.soccerField.setContentInset(self.currentInsets)
    }
}

@IBAction func horizontalNudgeButtonPressed() {
    if horizontalDirection == .Right {
        currentInsets.left += kickDistance

        if currentInsets.left + ballSize.width + kickDistance >
            soccerFieldSize.width {
            horizontalDirection = .Left
        }
    }
    else {
        currentInsets.left -= kickDistance

        if currentInsets.left - kickDistance < 0 {
            horizontalDirection = .Right
        }
    }

    animateWithDuration(kickDuration) {
        self.soccerField.setContentInset(self.currentInsets)
    }
}
```

These methods are pretty similar. By adjusting the insets from the top and the left, you can move the ball around the screen. If the ball is too close to the edge of the screen, you flip that direction, which resets the button's title and starts moving back the other way. Finally, in a call to animateWithDuration(duration:animations:), you animate this change.

Return to the storyboard and Control-drag from the buttons to the interface controller, connecting them to the appropriate outlets. Build and run the app and press the buttons. You'll see the ball move around inside the field. Now, WatchKit doesn't allow you to set the frame of an interface object directly, but, as you can see from this simple demo, the content inset of a group can get you pretty close to that functionality. Go ahead and play with the animation duration, the kick distance, or whatever you like.

Just like that, you made a simple animation-based game in about 100 lines of Swift using WKInterfaceGroup!

Wrap-Up

As you can see, groups in WatchKit let you unleash your creativity and solve all kinds of interesting UI problems. In this chapter, you learned how to use groups on their own and in buttons and how to nest groups to achieve your desired layout. Though it can get messy, using groups lets you do advanced positioning to get the precise user interface you want. One limitation to groups, however, is that all of their content has to be in your storyboard. What about apps that have dynamic content? You want TapALap to react to multiple runs and list them, as well as let the user select from multiple tracks. To do that, you need to use `WKInterfaceTable`, which takes groups one step further by allowing you to create dynamic content.

Delivering Dynamic Content with Tables

Every piece of user interface we've seen so far in WatchKit has something in common: it's static. We create the watch app's UI in Interface Builder, set it up just so, and then use it in the app, but we can't add or remove interface objects. Sure, we can get clever and hide some portions of the UI, but there's one thing we haven't yet seen: creating dynamic user interfaces that respond to users' data. In our iPhone app, we can create these interfaces manually, perhaps placed inside a UIScrollView if there's more than a screenful of content, but it's much more common—and easier—to use either UITableView or UICollectionView. WatchKit targets much smaller screen sizes than UIKit, so it offers us WKInterfaceTable, a simpler, stripped-down version of UIKit's table views.

In this chapter, let's explore tables in WatchKit. We'll cover how they work, how they differ from UIKit, and how to use them the right way. By the end of this chapter, you'll know how to present your data in rows, how to make it perform well, and how to make it look fantastic.

Comparing WatchKit Tables and iOS Table Views

If table views on iOS have one thing going for them, it's that they're routine fodder for introductory materials. Table views are where most developers new to working with Apple platforms encounter the delegation design pattern. Delegation is a routine stumbling block, most often encountered in UITableView. WKInterfaceTable, by contrast, has no datasource to set and no delegate to implement, and—most importantly—it eschews UIKit's "don't call us; we'll call you" paradigm in favor of requiring you to tell it in advance all of the data it'll need to display. If you've never used UITableView and have no idea what I'm talking about, don't worry. You don't need to have used it to understand WKInterfaceTable.

The difference between the two, as with many features of the Apple Watch UI, is that the display is divorced from the data. Your users scroll through content on the watch, and given its performance concerns, achieving the 60-frames-per-second scrolling users have come to expect from Apple devices requires tradeoffs. Instead of running code every time a new row comes onscreen, as you do with UITableView, you'll populate the entire table at once, allowing the watch's processor to take a break while the user moves the content up and down. This also helps battery life—another paramount concern for Apple Watch apps.

Architectural differences aside, you'll notice as soon as you drag a WKInterfaceTable onto the storyboard that each distinct type of row in the table is nothing more than a WKInterfaceGroup. Unlike UIKit's UITableViewCell, there's no built-in UI element to repurpose. Your table view rows will be fully custom groups, configured with whatever interface objects make sense. To serve as a bridge between your interface controller and your table rows, you'll create objects that coordinate the data, known as *row controllers*. Now, what to put in a table? To introduce using tables to show data, let's create a new screen in TapALap—one for displaying the user's run history in the app.

Row Types and Storyboard Groups

Every WKInterfaceTable delivers content to the user in vertically stacked rows. To demonstrate this, let's create a new interface controller in our running app. Once the user is finished with a run, she'll want to be able to quickly scroll through a history of her runs, comparing distances and paces as she goes. To that end, let's make an interface controller with a table in it that displays one row for each run, with the newest at the top.

First, open your watch app's storyboard and drag in a new interface controller. Give it the title "Run Log." Next, create a new WKInterfaceController subclass and name it RunLogInterfaceController, being sure to add it to your WatchKit extension and not your iPhone app. You'll come back and implement some methods later on, but for now you just need the class to exist. Head back to the storyboard and select the interface controller you just made. In Xcode's Identity Inspector, under Custom Class, set the Class value to RunLogInterfaceController. Now your storyboard and your subclass are in sync. Finally, drag the Main arrow to the interface controller so the app starts right at that screen.

To implement the UI, you'll need to head over to the Object Library and drag a new WKInterfaceTable, listed simply as Table, onto the interface controller. By default, it has one group inside. Each row type in the table is represented by a group in your storyboard; the table will re-create that group for every row of that type. For this row, you want to show the user the run's date, distance, and duration. You'll use three WKInterfaceLabel objects for it and arrange them in the group. As you saw in the chapter on groups, you can use subgroups to arrange these labels nicely, and that's what you're going to do.

First, create the three labels by dragging them from Xcode's Object Library to the row group. To help keep track of them as you lay them out, you'll give them custom titles. In the Document Outline of the storyboard (if you don't see it on the left side of the storyboard, click Editor → Show Document Outline), you can press ↵ and change the display name of a selected item. Instead of Label, name these "Date Label," "Distance Label," and "Duration Label." Now you can see what you're doing. The result you want is the date label in large, bold text above the distance label, with the duration label on the right side. To that end, select both date and distance labels and select Editor → Embed In → Vertical Group. The duration label disappears; since the vertical group is by default set to match the width of its container, it pushes everything else away. Select the new group and, in Xcode's Attributes Inspector, change its width to Size To Fit Content. Now you'll see all three on the same screen.

Select the duration label, change its font to the built-in Subhead style, and set its horizontal position to Right. Change the date label's font to the Headline style and the distance label's font to the Footnote style. Now your row is looking pretty good, if a bit stretched out. There's a lot of vertical space, so select the group that contains the left two labels, open the Attributes Inspector, and give it a custom spacing of 0. Now that you've done all this, your interface controller in the storyboard should look like the following image.

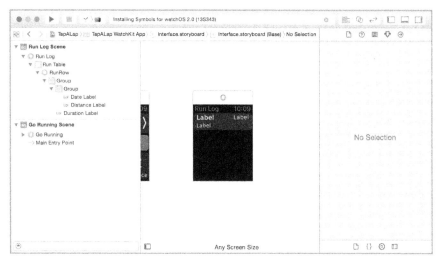

Snazzy! After admiring your handiwork for a bit, you can start putting real data into this row and see how it works. To do that, you need to create a row controller object.

Linking Content to the UI with Row Controllers

Looking at the interface object hierarchy in the storyboard's Run Log interface controller (if you don't see it, select Editor → Show Document Outline), you can see that your labels are nested inside a parent group, but that instead of the group being a child of the table (which would match how it appears in the interface editor), there's an intermediate object that looks different, called Table Row Controller. This is the row controller we've been talking about, and it's vital to understanding how tables work in WatchKit.

Row controllers are lightweight objects that sit between tables and row content. Their entire role is to ferry data from your interface controller to the interface objects you've set up in the storyboard. Your row controller is going to be incredibly simple, let's create it now and walk through what it needs to do.

You'll need a new class for the row controller, and since you'll be referencing it from the storyboard, it'll need to inherit from NSObject—storyboards use a lot of internal NSObject magic. Name the class RunLogRowController. Create a new Swift file called RunLogRowController.swift using the WatchKit Class template to create the class.

Next, let's set up outlets for your UI elements. You'll make one for each label (there's no need to reference their containing groups for now), and name them the same as they're named in the storyboard:

Chapter 5/TapALap/TapALap WatchKit Extension/RunLogRowController.swift

```
@IBOutlet weak var dateLabel: WKInterfaceLabel!
@IBOutlet weak var distanceLabel: WKInterfaceLabel!
@IBOutlet weak var durationLabel: WKInterfaceLabel!
```

With that set up, you need to connect these outlets to your UI so that you can reference the interface objects in code. Head back to the storyboard and select the row controller object in the Run Log interface controller's Document Outline. In Xcode's Identity Inspector, change its class to RunLogRowController. In the Attributes Inspector, set its Identifier to RunRow. If you fail to do this, the table won't be able to create the row, because it uses this identifier to, well, identify it. Now you can link it up with its outlets. For each label, Control-drag from the row controller in the Document Outline to the label, selecting the appropriate outlet.

Your UI is all hooked up and you need to put the appropriate data in it. To keep the row controller class separate from your model objects, the row controller will deal only with values: distance, duration, and date. Add a new method, configure(date:distance:duration:), and it will take care of the UI for you:

```swift
var dateFormatter: NSDateFormatter?
var distanceFormatter: NSLengthFormatter?
var durationFormatter: NSDateComponentsFormatter?

func configure(date date: NSDate, distance: Double, duration: NSTimeInterval) {
    dateLabel.setText(dateFormatter?.stringFromDate(date))
    distanceLabel.setText(distanceFormatter?.stringFromMeters(distance))
    durationLabel.setText(durationFormatter?.stringFromTimeInterval(duration))
}
```

When a new RunLogRowController is created, the dateFormatter, distanceFormatter, and durationFormatter properties are all nil. These are all NSFormatter subclasses to help you convert numbers to strings, but instead of creating them in this class, you'll fill them in later—that way you can reuse your NSDateFormatter.

Perfect. Whenever you call configure(date:distance:duration:), you'll automatically put the data into your UI. That raises the next question: when does that happen? Let's look at the other side of this and get some data into your table.

Configuring the Content in Tables

Now that you've squared away how your row controller is going to behave, you can use it in your RunLogInterfaceController. Unlike UITableView from UIKit, where you'd return the number of rows from a data source method and then configure each row on demand, you'll set the number of rows manually and then iterate through them and configure them as you go. You'll also configure your NSFormatter subclasses to do formatting and then pass them to each row controller. You'll get everything set up in the interface controller's willActivate() method. First, however, you need the data to put in the rows. Add a new Swift file to your WatchKit extension, and name it Run.swift. In it, create a new class with some properties for a run:

```swift
class Run {
    let distance: Double // in meters
    let laps: [NSTimeInterval]
    let startDate: NSDate

    init(distance: Double, laps: [NSTimeInterval], startDate: NSDate) {
        self.distance = distance
        self.laps = laps
        self.startDate = startDate
    }
}
```

Joe asks:
Why Do We Need to Reuse Date Formatters?

Creating a date formatter, according to Apple's Data Formatting Guide, "is not a cheap operation."[a] If we were to create a new date formatter for every row in the table, we'd be sitting here for a long time waiting for a table of any reasonable length to display. Speed is the name of the game with tables (see Performance Concerns, on page 54, for more), so we want our code to be as efficient as possible.

---

a. From Apple's Data Formatting Guide at developer.apple.com/library/prerelease/watchos/
documentation/Cocoa/Conceptual/DataFormatting/Articles/dfDateFormatting10_4.html#//apple_ref/
doc/uid/TP40002369-SW10.

You could have made Run a struct instead, but you'll be using it for some class-only functionality in the future, so marking it as a class now avoids future headaches. Now that you have the class to store the data, head back to RunLogInterfaceController.swift and add an array of runs to display:

```
var runs: [Run]?
```

Before you can add rows to the table, you need a way to reference it. Open the storyboard and the Assistant Editor, and then connect the table in your Run Log interface controller to a new @IBOutlet property called runTable:

```
@IBOutlet weak var runTable: WKInterfaceTable!
```

Connecting the @IBOutlet is especially easy using the Assistant Editor; simply click the circle to the left of its declaration; then drag to the table in your UI, just as in this image:

You're now ready to display run data in the table. In the interface controller's willActivate() method, you'll iterate over the runs array:

Chapter 5/TapALap/TapALap WatchKit Extension/RunLogInterfaceController.swift

```
Line 1  override func willActivate() {
            super.willActivate()

            guard let runs = runs else { return }
    5
            runTable.setNumberOfRows(runs.count, withRowType: "RunRow")

            for i in 0 ..< runTable.numberOfRows {
                guard let rowController = runTable.rowControllerAtIndex(i)
   10               as? RunLogRowController else { continue }

                configureRow(rowController, forRun: runs[i])
            }
        }
```

You get started with the table on line 6, when you set the number of rows to the number of runs in your runs array. Then you get to a for loop on line 8, and this is where the real fun begins. The table tells you how many row controllers it created with its numberOfRows() method, so you can loop through them. Inside each loop, you call the table's rowControllerAtIndex() method to get the row controller it's created for the row, and then you can modify it—but before you can use it, you need to make sure it's the right class, because rowControllerAtIndex() returns AnyObject?.

To do that, you'll create a method called configureRow(_:forRun:). In that method, you simply pass in your formatters and the proper Run instance, and the code you wrote in the section on row configuration, on page 47, runs to configure the row. Here's what the method should look like:

Chapter 6/TapALap/TapALap WatchKit Extension/RunLogInterfaceController.swift

```
func configureRow(rowController: RunLogRowController, forRun run: Run) {
    rowController.dateFormatter = dateFormatter
    rowController.distanceFormatter = distanceFormatter
    rowController.durationFormatter = durationFormatter

    rowController.configure(date: run.startDate,
        distance: run.distance,
        duration: run.duration)
}
```

That method was easy. If you try to build, you'll notice that you never declared the formatters, so let's do that now. You don't need them to be created until you actually use them, so lazy variables in Swift are a perfect match. Head up to the class extension and add some declarations for them:

Chapter 5/TapALap/TapALap WatchKit Extension/RunLogInterfaceController.swift

```
lazy var dateFormatter: NSDateFormatter = {
    let dateFormatter = NSDateFormatter()
    dateFormatter.dateStyle = .ShortStyle
    return dateFormatter
}()

lazy var distanceFormatter = NSLengthFormatter()

lazy var durationFormatter: NSDateComponentsFormatter = {
    let dateComponentsFormatter = NSDateComponentsFormatter()
    dateComponentsFormatter.unitsStyle = .Positional
    return dateComponentsFormatter
}()
```

Now that you've declared them, you can use them whenever they're needed, and because they're marked lazy, they'll be initialized the first time they're used. Note that two of them need more customization, so wrap the customizations in a closure, using its return value as the initialized value of the property. Next, you need a duration property for the Run class, which you can create as a computed property. The duration of the run is the same as the sum of all of its laps, so you can use Swift's reduce() method to add them:

Chapter 5/TapALap/TapALap WatchKit Extension/Run.swift

```
var duration: NSTimeInterval {
    return laps.reduce(0, combine: +)
}
```

You're finished! Build and run the app, and the content of your runs array will be displayed in the run log. Only there isn't anything in that array. For now, you can add some test data:

Chapter 5/TapALap/TapALap WatchKit Extension/RunLogInterfaceController.swift

```
override init() {
    srand48(time(UnsafeMutablePointer<time_t>(bitPattern: 0)))

    let randomRun: (NSDate) -> Run = { date in
        let lapCount = arc4random_uniform(20) + 5
        let lapDistance = arc4random_uniform(1000) + 1

        var laps: [NSTimeInterval] = []

        for _ in 0 ..< lapCount {
            // Pace is in m/s. 9 minutes per mile is about 3 meters per second.
            // Generate a random pace between ~7.5 min/mi and ~10.5 min/mi.
            let speed = 3.0 + (drand48() - 0.5) // in meters per second
            let lapDuration: NSTimeInterval = Double(lapDistance) / speed

            laps.append(lapDuration)
        }
```

```
    let run = Run(distance: Double(lapDistance * lapCount),
        laps: laps,
        startDate: date)

    return run
}

runs = []

for i in 0 ..< 5 {
    runs?.append(randomRun(NSDate().dateByAddingTimeInterval(Double(i)
        * 24 * 60 * 60)))
}
}
```

For real this time, you can display data. Build and run one more time and you'll see something like this:

As you can see, getting your data into the table is pretty straightforward. If you needed to use multiple types of rows with different row controllers, you'd use the table's setRow-Types() method instead of setNumberOfRows(_:with-RowType:). To use that method, simply create an array of strings, one for each row in the table, set to the row type identifier. If you do that, keep in mind that the row controller class you get back from your table's rowControllerAtIndex() method will depend on that identifier! In your willActivate() you can assume you're getting a RunLogRowController, but in more complicated table layouts you won't be so lucky.

Another reason this code is so straightforward is that you have static content. You create the table in the storyboard and set the number of rows in your interface controller's code, and then you're finished with it. The watch takes care of scrolling for you, and everything is smooth as butter. If you need to *modify* the contents of the table, things get a bit trickier.

Modifying Tables

Whereas setting up a table's contents in WatchKit is markedly different from using UITableView on iOS, modifying the content once you've done that initial setup is pretty similar—you just need to tell the table where to add the rows. To support what you're going to do in the next chapter, let's include support for adding a new run to the table once you've set everything up.

You'll use the interface controller's awakeWithContext() method to receive the data. When you get a Run passed in as the context, you'll use the table's insertRowsAtIndexes(_:withRowType:) method to add the row. You'll then use its rowControllerAtIndex() just like when you set up the table, but this time just for the newly inserted row. Your method will look like this when you've finished:

```
Chapter 6/TapALap/TapALap WatchKit Extension/RunLogInterfaceController.swift
override func awakeWithContext(context: AnyObject?) {
    super.awakeWithContext(context)

    if let run = context as? Run {
        runs?.insert(run, atIndex: 0)

        runTable.insertRowsAtIndexes(NSIndexSet(index: 0),
            withRowType: "RunRow")

        if let rowc = runTable.rowControllerAtIndex(0) as? RunLogRowController {
            configureRow(rowc, forRun: run)
        }
    }
}
```

Thanks to the configureRow(_:forRun:) method we wrote, on page 49, you need to reuse very little code here. This is a pretty simple case, since you only need to add a row to the top of the table. You create an NSIndexSet to store the indexes of rows you need to add. If you're adding rows all over the place in your table, you may want to take advantage of NSIndexSet's enumerateIndexesUsing-Block(_:) method to iterate over your row controllers, as follows:

```
var indexSet: NSIndexSet // a complicated index set

table.insertRowsAtIndexes(indexSet, withRowType:"RowType")

indexSet.enumerateIndexesUsingBlock { index, _ in
    let rowController = table.rowControllerAtIndex(index)

    // configure row here
}
```

In this example, indexSet contains rows throughout the data set. You insert the rows into the table and then call enumerateIndexesUsingBlock(_:). This method runs the closure you pass into it once for each index in the index set. For each index, you'd configure a row controller.

It's important to make sure you always get the row controller for the proper index(es), and the preceding technique can help you avoid mistakes. As with setting up content for the first time, this example was pretty easy because the rows are all of the same type. If you need to insert rows of multiple types, you'll need to call insertRowsAtIndexes(_:withRowType:) for *each* row type; there's no method to add multiple row types in one go.

Deleting rows from the table is much the same as inserting them, but you don't need to do any work once they're gone. Simply call removeRowsAtIndexes() with an index set, and your table will automatically remove the rows and destroy the associated row controllers for you. You can call this method no matter what the row types are for the rows in question.

That's all there is to modifying the content of the table once it's set up. You can insert and delete rows, but unlike with UITableView on iPhone, there are no facilities to reorder rows, nor is there any swipe-to-delete functionality. The only way to get user input from a table is to have the user tap it. Let's explore that next.

Considering Table Input

If you look at the documentation for WKInterfaceTable, you may notice that there is no delegate property nor (seemingly) any way to handle when the user taps your table. Is this some massive oversight of WatchKit? Do you need to search for a cryptic informal protocol in Objective-C? Turns out the answer is no for both questions. When the user interacts with a WKInterfaceTable, those interactions are *automatically* forwarded to the table's containing interface controller, much like the responder chain automatically forwards touch events on iOS. Specifically, you want to look at WKInterfaceController's table(_:didSelectRowAtIndex:) method, which watchOS will call whenever the user taps a row.

In your table, you'll probably want to show the details for a run when the user taps a row. We'll cover displaying another interface controller later, so for now let's just display a message so you know it works. Implement table(_:didSelectRowAtIndex:) like so:

Chapter 5/TapALap/TapALap WatchKit Extension/RunLogInterfaceController.swift

```swift
override func table(table: WKInterfaceTable,
    didSelectRowAtIndex rowIndex: Int) {
        NSLog("User tapped on row \(rowIndex)")
}
```

Build, run and then tap a row. You'll see the log message appear in the console in Xcode. In a real app, you'd want to do something with this action, but this is enough to see how simple it is to interact with table rows in your app.

Some apps will require more advanced layouts than simple rows. If you add a button, switch, slider, or other interactive control to your table row, you'll need to use action methods on those objects. When the user taps an interface object that can accept a tap, your table(_:didSelectRowAtIndex:) method is not called. This affords you some extra ways to interact with your app, but it can be more complicated and a bit harder to use. If you add interface objects that receive taps, such as buttons or switches, to the row, those objects will receive taps when the user taps them. If the user taps *outside* those interface objects but still on your row, then watchOS will call your table(_:didSelectRowAtIndex:) method. Since you're dealing with such small screens here, it's best to keep the table row to a limited set of controls—preferably two at most, including tapping the row itself.

Performance Concerns

The most fundamental differences between WKInterfaceTable and UITableView relate to the way row content is set up. The interesting thing about WatchKit's approach here is that it's in direct contrast with the way iOS does it, and yet UIKit on iOS works the way it does for performance reasons. You'd think the lowest power device—Apple Watch—would have the most efficient API for table performance, but the needs are quite different.

The WKInterfaceTable API remains virtually unchanged from watchOS 1. You may recall that in WatchKit for watchOS 1, every time a method is called in your WatchKit extension and the watch UI is updated, Bluetooth communication is happening between the watch and the phone. If WKInterfaceTable were to use the same API as UITableView, then the watch and phone would be in constant communication while the user scrolled the table. That would have a huge battery-life penalty, so instead all the data is communicated at once and cached on the watch, and WatchKit takes care of drawing the table while the user scrolls. Even though under watchOS 2 the processing for the app is happening on the watch device itself, this API was built to accommodate the previous OS paradigm.

What does this mean for the performance of your app? For one, you should be very careful to limit the number of rows in your table. Your code right now simply uses the runs array to determine the number of rows. For this app that's probably fine at first, but what happens if a user runs every day, religiously, using your app for, say, five years, and is still using his first-gen Apple Watch? Now you'd have almost 2,000 runs to deal with at once. Chances are your user won't need access to all of his runs. It might be smart to limit the number of runs you display at once to 25 or 50. That way, the user can still see relevant, timely data, but you don't spend a lot of his time (and battery life) on rendering content he's probably never going to look at. Think about cases like this and try to minimize the amount of work the watch needs to do, and your users will thank you for it.

Wrap-Up

Phew! Tables are where WatchKit apps start to get a bit more complicated, huh? You're out of the land of canned UIs for everything and starting to do some real work. Your app still has one pretty big drawback, however: you can't go from screen to screen. You probably don't always want to be on the Run Log interface controller. In the next chapter, we'll look at how you can transition between interface controllers.

Navigating Between Interfaces

You've seen a lot of interface controllers by now, but they've all been self-contained and haven't transitioned from one to another. While it's certainly possible to build an app with one interface controller, a Glance, and notification handlers, it wouldn't be very exciting. Your data probably won't all fit on one screen, nor would your users appreciate an app where all of the content is crammed into one screen that requires tons of scrolling. Before you can break up your content into multiple interface controllers, you need to learn how to move between them.

In this chapter you'll learn about the different segues you can implement to transition between interface controllers, as well as the different ways to display them. We'll discuss the relationship between interface controllers as laid out in your storyboard (and the segues between them) and your code, as well as how to manage resources. By the end of the chapter, you'll be able to provide a list of interface controllers for your users to page through, present interface controllers modally when you need user input before proceeding, and present interface controllers in a hierarchical layout. To send data around in the app, you'll be able to use the interface controllers' contexts as they're created.

Linking Interfaces in Your Storyboard

There are several ways to go from one interface controller to another. You'll see them as the chapter goes on, but one thing to note right away is that whether you're performing the transition in code or linking it up in Interface Builder, every interface controller must have its user interface laid out in your storyboard file. Unlike your iPhone app, where you can create view objects from code, from a storyboard, or from a .xib, every single UI element needs to exist in your storyboard *before* it's referenced.

Another departure from UIKit on iPhone is that WatchKit includes a built-in way to pass *context* from one interface controller to another. The context you pass can be model objects, raw data, or nothing at all, but the ability to send this context is a nice way to distribute data without having to implement new methods in each view controller. You'll see just how handy this can be later on, when you structure your app. For now, let's look at the simplest way to move from one screen to another: linking them together in the storyboard. You don't even need to write any code!

One of the simplest ways to navigate an iPhone app is to use UINavigationController to create a hierarchy of view controllers, the topmost of which is onscreen. You push a new view controller onto the stack to display it, and you pop it off to go back (or when your user taps the Back button). This is a well-understood way to dive into hierarchical data, and it's easy to implement on the watch, as well. Let's try it out.

Pushing an Interface Controller

Open the TapALap app's storyboard. To make it easy, drag your interface controllers around so that your Go Running interface controller is to the left of your Run Log interface controller. Drop a new WKInterfaceButton onto your Go Running interface controller and title it "Run Log." You want this button to open the run log, so Control-drag from the button to your Run Log interface controller. When you release the mouse button, a pop-up named Action Segue will appear, with two choices for the type of segue you'd like to create: Push or Modal. Consult the images here to make sure you've connected it properly:

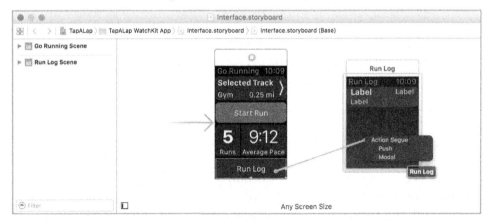

To achieve the navigation controller–like effect, choose Push. This causes your interface controller to "push" the new interface controller onto the stack. Run your project with ⌘R to see how it works. When you run your app, it should look like the image here. The left-facing chevron indicates that there's an interface controller to return to; tapping it or swiping left to right from the watch's edge will return to the original one. Try it out both ways!

Using just this knowledge, you can already create pretty complicated interfaces. It's fairly common for iPhone apps to drill down several layers deep in a hierarchy to get to the data you want to interact with, but with the limited screen real estate and interaction model of Apple Watch, you should use restraint. Nobody wants to page back through five layers of interface controllers on their wrist. When used appropriately, however, pushing new interface controllers makes a convenient, understandable structure of your interface controllers. This Run Log button seems unnecessary for your app, though, doesn't it? Let's try a different way of linking these together so that the user doesn't even need to push a button to go from one to another.

Using Paged Interface Controllers

If you look at the list of Glances on your watch, you'll see that each one is on its own screen, and to navigate between them you simply swipe left or right. There's a page indicator on the bottom of the screen to show you which page you're on, and it's another familiar interface for iPhone users. WatchKit, however, doesn't require you to use UIPageViewController and its cumbersome data source methods. Instead, you can lay out your interface controllers in the storyboard and get both the ability to swipe between them and the automatically updating page indicator for free—and still without writing a single line of code!

Head back to your storyboard and delete the Run Log button. You never needed it anyway. Notice that arrow pointing to your Go Running interface controller? That signifies that this is the first interface controller to be loaded when your user starts the watch app. To set up paging between view controllers, you don't need to add a new, higher-level interface controller or add any fancy structure to the app. Simply Control-drag from the Go Running interface controller to the Run Log interface controller, just as you did for the button. Now, however, the list of possible segues is different; its title is Relationship Segue, and the only option is Next Page. Select it and your interfaces will be linked together, as shown in the image on page 60.

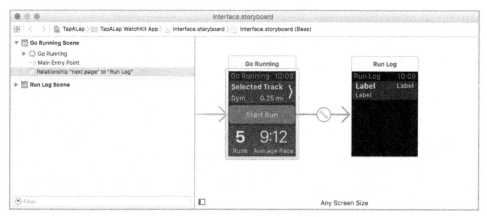

Build and run the app, and notice that you now have a page indicator on the bottom of the screen. Swipe right to left and you'll see your Run Log interface (see the right side of the same image), no extra work required.

This is much better for what you're trying to accomplish with your app. You want the default screen to be Go Running, since that's what most users will open the app to do, but you also want to have the log quickly accessible. You could have stuck with the Run Log button, but a hierarchical interface implies some kind of ownership or parent-child relationship between the two controllers. That kind of relationship doesn't exist between these two interface controllers. Since they make more sense as siblings than as a parent and child, you put them side-by-side and let the user navigate freely.

All is not rosy in the world of paged and pushed interface controllers, however. To illustrate, let's add the next interface controller to your interface. From the Run Log interface controller, you want to view a run's details when the user taps it. When that happens, you want to display a new interface controller with that run's details. We'll cover getting the run details set up later in this chapter, on page 74, but for now we can tackle presenting the interface.

Drag a new interface controller into your storyboard. Give it the title "Run Details." Next, create a new WKInterfaceController subclass for it called RunDetailsInterfaceController. You don't need to set anything up yet, so you can leave it as the stock Xcode template. Head back to the storyboard and enter RunDetailsInterfaceController into the new interface controller's Class property in Xcode's Identity Inspector.

As with the first transition you made, you want the Run Details interface controller to appear when the user taps. This time, however, you want the tap to be on a row in the table, not a button. To accomplish this, Control-drag from the run log's row-controller object to the Run Details interface controller.

This will connect the individual row—and therefore the individual run—to the new interface controller. Also like before, select Push for your segue. You'll now have three interfaces lined up, as in the image here.

Build and run the app. You can still page from one interface controller to the next, as before. Tap a row in the Run Log interface controller and *nothing happens*. What have you done wrong? As it turns out, these two types of interface navigation are mutually exclusive. You can't push into a paged interface controller, nor can you push *from* one. If you think about it, it makes sense—if you swiped left to right to go back from a pushed interface controller to paged interface controllers and then swiped in that same direction, you'd be navigating between pages, not going back. Whereas paging and pushing—on their own—are well-understood navigation idioms on both the watch and other iOS devices, mixing the two is not and can cause confusion on your users' part. Fortunately, WatchKit won't let you do this.

So how are you supposed to display these run details? You don't want to add a new interface controller to your existing pages for every run the user takes. Eventually that would become impossible to navigate. You also don't want to return to pushing the run log from the Go Running interface controller; we've already established that the paging interface is better. Fear not! There's a third option: you can present the details modally.

Presenting Modal Interfaces

Let's go back to the storyboard. Instead of deleting the segue, you can simply change its type. Click the segue that links the Run Log and the Run Details interface controllers and open Xcode's Attributes Inspector. In the drop-down labeled Segue, you can change the type. Select Modal, and the segue's icon will change. It should now look like the following image on page 62. Build and run the app, and you should see the Run Details interface controller appear when you tap a row in the Run Log interface controller.

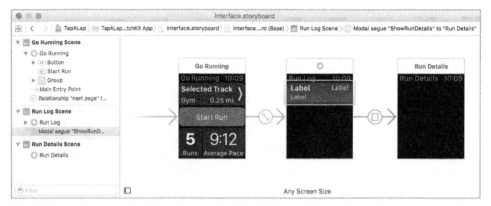

Modal interface controllers look slightly different than the other variety. For one, the title is stark white instead of the usual gray. Second, the time has disappeared from the status bar and the page indicator is gone. In fact, as you can see in the image here, the interface controller is pretty bare:

This modal presentation isn't quite as user friendly as the previous two presentation styles. The title is white to indicate that it's turned into a close button; tap it to dismiss the interface controller. To make this clearer to the user, let's do one final tweak: select the Run Details interface controller in your storyboard, open the Attributes Inspector in Xcode, and delete its title. Build and run again, and you'll notice that WatchKit, in the absence of a title, chooses Cancel. This is appropriate for when you're presenting a modal interface controller to perform an action, but since you're just displaying data, Cancel doesn't have much contextual meaning. Change the title to Close, and you'll be more closely describing what's actually happening.

While modal interface controllers have their caveats, they can be pretty important in your watch app. Whether you need to break out of a paged interface to present some information, present pages of information from within a pushed hierarchy, or interrupt the user so she can perform an action, a modal interface controller is sometimes necessary.

Interface Transitions in Code

Not every transition can be implemented in your storyboard. Whether you need to gut your app's interface entirely and start fresh or dynamically choose interface controllers to present, you may need to use some of WKInterfaceCon-troller's methods to accomplish your tasks. Because of this, you may see interface controllers in your storyboard that don't appear to be connected to anything. Fear not: you can always instantiate one by name, using the iden-tifier that you give it in the storyboard. For that reason, Xcode will warn you if you have an interface controller in your storyboard with no linked segues or an identifier—there's no way to get to it! Let's look at two ways to transition in code. First, let's transition when the user taps a button.

Presenting an Interface Controller

Remember the button you created to configure the track on the Go Running interface controller? Tapping it should probably transition to a screen on which you can configure a track. To accomplish that, you'll need a new interface controller. Select File → New → File in Xcode, choose WatchKit Class in the templates, and make a new subclass of WKInterfaceController named Track-ConfigurationInterfaceController. Once you've added the interface controller to your project, you can add a new interface controller to the storyboard and use the Identity Inspector to set its class to TrackConfigurationInterfaceController. Instead of making a segue from the button to the interface controller, to do it in code you need to give the interface controller an identifier. Open the Attributes Inspector, select the new interface controller, and give it the identifier "TrackConfiguration." Since you're going to present it modally, you'll leave the interface controller's title blank.

To perform this transition in code, first you need to add a new method to GoRunningInterfaceController.swift:

Chapter 6/TapALap/TapALap WatchKit Extension/GoRunningInterfaceController.swift

```
@IBAction func trackButtonPressed() {
    presentControllerWithName("TrackConfiguration", context: self)
}
```

Rather than creating the interface controller in code, this method simply calls presentControllerWithName(_:context:) with a string. This string is the identifier you set in your storyboard, so be sure that they match!

All that's left is to configure the button to call this method when you tap it. Head back to your Interface.storyboard and Control-drag from the Selected Track button to the Go Running interface controller, and then select trackButtonPressed() from the pop-up. Build and run, tap the button, and you'll see the new interface controller! It doesn't do anything yet, but you'll fix that later. For your next code-based transition, you'll use a more complicated process and reload the entire app's interface.

Reloading the Interface

The main point of your app is to time users while they run laps at the track, but none of these presentation methods you've seen so far seem appropriate. The Go Running interface is a likely place to start, but it has more to do with selecting a track than doing the timing, and having it do both would make it needlessly complex. You could add a new interface controller to the end of the list, but what would it look like when your users are not on a run? Furthermore, do you really want your users inspecting their run logs while they're on the track? I, for one, would prefer they keep their eyes in front of them to avoid accidents. At my local gym, much of the track is on a second-floor balcony overlooking the basketball courts, and I certainly don't want my users' eyes glued to their wrist while they're navigating those turns up there.

To avoid all of these problems, when a user starts a run, you'll replace the user interface in its entirety. While a run is active, the lap timer will be the *only* screen accessible to the user. When the user stops a run, you'll come back to the existing user interface. This kind of transition can't be done in the storyboard, so you need to write some code.

Return to your Go Running interface controller in Interface.storyboard. Open Xcode's Assistant Editor to GoRunningInterfaceController.swift and connect it to a new IBAction method in your GoRunningInterfaceController class by Control-dragging from the button to the implementation file. Call it startRunButtonPressed() (to see how to connect an @IBAction this way, consult the figure on page 65).

To implement startRunButtonPressed(), you need a reference to a RunTimerInterfaceController instance that will become the new interface. You can't create it directly as you would other classes by calling RunTimerInterfaceController() or some other initializer, though, since all WatchKit user interface objects—even interface controllers—must come from the storyboard. Instead, you have to reference it through its storyboard identifier. Open the storyboard, give it the identifier "RunTimer", then return to GoRunningInterfaceController and use it:

Chapter 6/TapALap/TapALap WatchKit Extension/GoRunningInterfaceController.swift

```
@IBAction func startRunButtonPressed() {
    let names = ["RunTimer"]

    WKInterfaceController.reloadRootControllersWithNames(names,
        contexts: nil)
}
```

Once you have the identifier that the storyboard uses as the interface controller's name, it's straightforward to change your interface. Notice that the first parameter of reloadRootControllersWithNames(_:contexts:) is an Array. This allows

Figure 2—Creating an @IBAction method by dragging from storyboard to the Swift file

you to pass multiple names and switch to a page-based layout. You simply provide the controllers in the order you'd like them to appear. For your needs, you just pack the one name into an array and pass it along. Don't worry about the contexts parameter yet; you'll see more about passing data later in this chapter on page 74.

Build and run the app; then press the Start Run button. You'll be whisked away magically to your RunTimerInterfaceController. The page indicator at the bottom of the screen is gone, because you're now viewing only the one interface controller, just as you wanted. Unfortunately, there's no cancel button, nor can you swipe to go back. You need to provide your users a way to go back to where they started, and it'll have to be in code. You'll probably want to do this when the user ends a run, so let's give them a way to do just that. Modify the endRun() method accordingly:

```
func endRun() {
let names = ["GoRunning", "RunLog"]

WKInterfaceController.reloadRootControllersWithNames(names,
    contexts: nil)
}
```

Be sure to go into Interface.storyboard and give these interface controllers the identifiers "GoRunning" and "RunLog," respectively. Tapping End Run will now take you back to where you began. As you can see, when you need to transition between interface controllers in code, it can get a bit more complicated than when you do it in the storyboard, but either way gets you where you need to go.

You're not *quite* finished here, however. When the user taps End Run, she goes back to the Go Running screen because that's the first interface controller in your list. It's pretty unlikely that the user will want to go running again immediately after finishing, so wouldn't it be more useful to jump directly to the run log? Let's see how to do exactly that.

Passing Data Between Interfaces

To navigate directly to the Run Log page when a run is done, you need to call becomeCurrentPage() of your RunLogInterfaceController. When you go back to it by calling reloadRootControllersWithNames(_:contexts:), you're just passing the name of the controller to WKInterfaceController. You don't get back any references to the new interface controller, so how can you call becomeCurrentPage() on it?

One approach might be to use NSNotificationCenter. After you reload the controllers, you could send a notification with a short delay and then listen for that notification in your RunLogInterfaceController and call becomeCurrentPage(). That would probably work, but there's a better way. Remember the contexts parameter we were ignoring earlier? What the heck is that, anyway?

Passing Contexts in Code

Whenever you create an interface controller, you have the opportunity to pass it some *context*, which can be anything you want (or nothing at all). Because you don't create interface controllers directly yourself, you can't create different initializer methods. You could imagine, for instance, that you might solve this problem by creating a new convenience initializer on RunLogInterfaceController:

```
convenience init(becomeCurrentPage: Bool) {
  self.init()

  if becomeCurrentPage {
    self.becomeCurrentPage()
  }
}
```

The merits of actually *doing* it that way aside, you can't make a custom initializer, so it's a moot point—remember, you can only create interface objects (and interface controllers) in the storyboard. Instead, you can pass a custom context object so that you can respond to it in the awakeWithContext() method of your interface controller. First, let's amend the endRun() method in RunTimer-InterfaceController.swift:

Chapter 6/TapALap/TapALap WatchKit Extension/RunTimerInterfaceController.swift

```
func endRun() {
    let names = ["GoRunning", "RunLog"]

    let contexts: [AnyObject]?

    if let lapTimes = lapTimes, startDate = startDate {
        let distance = track.lapDistance * Double(lapTimes.count)

        let run = Run(distance: distance,
            laps: lapTimes,
            startDate: startDate)

        contexts = [NSNull(), run]
    }
    else {
        contexts = nil
    }

    WKInterfaceController.reloadRootControllersWithNames(names,
        contexts: contexts)
}
```

For the second item in the contexts, you'll pass the Run object representing the run that you just finished. That NSNull is there to fill space; since the second controller in the names array receives the second context in the contexts array, you need to give *something* to the first one. nil can't be in an Array, so NSNull saves the day by allowing you to put an empty placeholder there. All that aside, once you pass the run to the RunLogInterfaceController, you need to handle it on the other side. Open RunLogInterfaceController.swift and add a line to awakeWith-Context() that calls becomeCurrentPage():

```
override func awakeWithContext(context: AnyObject?) {
    super.awakeWithContext(context)

    if let run = context as? Run {
        runs?.insert(run, atIndex: 0)

        runTable.insertRowsAtIndexes(NSIndexSet(index: 0),
            withRowType: "RunRow")

        if let rowc = runTable.rowControllerAtIndex(0) as? RunLogRowController {
            configureRow(rowc, forRun: run)
        }

        becomeCurrentPage()
    }
}
```

Build and run your app; you'll be navigated right back to the run log after completing a run. Neat! That's not all the context parameter can do, however, and you're in the right place to use it some more. By passing model objects around, you can use it to configure your Run Detail interface controller for an individual run.

Passing Contexts Through Storyboard Segues

Earlier, on page 61, when you configured your run log to display the Run Details interface controller, you used a storyboard segue to display the controller. You didn't even write any code, so how are you going to send any context data? WKInterfaceController has your back with the contextForSegueWithIdentifier(_:inTable:rowIndex:) method. If you implement this method, it'll be called as you select the run to display, and you can return a context that'll get passed to the segue's destination. Unlike with an iPhone app, where you'd get a reference to the UIStoryboardSegue itself and could access its destinationViewController to determine which segue this is, with WatchKit you get only the segue's identifier. Let's fill that in first.

Head over to the watch app's storyboard and select the modal segue between the Run Log interface controller and the Run Details interface controller. Open Xcode's Attributes Inspector and give the segue the identifier "ShowRunDetails." Now that you can properly identify the segue, let's pass some context along. Open RunLogInterfaceController.swift and implement contextForSegueWithIdentifier(_:inTable:rowIndex:):

```swift
override func contextForSegueWithIdentifier(segueIdentifier: String,
    inTable table: WKInterfaceTable, rowIndex: Int) -> AnyObject? {
        if segueIdentifier == "ShowRunDetails" {
            guard let runs = runs where runs.count > rowIndex else {
                return nil
            }

            return runs[rowIndex]
        }

        return nil
}
```

Compare the segue's identifier with the one you set up in the storyboard; this checks whether the segue in question is the one you're concerned with. If it is, the context you return is the run for that row, so pull it out of your runs array and send it over. For other segues, or if the index is out of bounds for your array, you'll return nil. Next up is displaying the details of a single run.

Implementing Run Details

The RunDetailsInterfaceController class will be pretty simple, showing details for a run, down to individual lap times. In the storyboard, drag in a label and then two groups. Change the label's text to "Run Date" so you can find it later, and then create a new @IBOutlet for it, named runDateLabel.

Change the layout of the first group to Horizontal. Add two labels, naming them "Distance" and "Pace," and set the latter's Horizontal position in Xcode to Right. Connect them to outlets named runDistanceLabel and runPaceLabel.

In the second group, add a label and name it "Laps:" (with the colon). This will serve as a header of sorts for the next item: a table. In the table's row controller, add three labels, giving them the titles "Lap," "0," and "0:00:00," respectively. Change the font of the middle label to Headline; this will be the number of the lap as the table is filled in. Change the 0:00:00 label on the right to be right-aligned. Connect the table to an outlet called lapsTable.

As with any row controller, you'll need a new class for it. Rather than making a new Swift file, you can declare it in RunDetailsInterfaceController.swift, indicating that the class "belongs" to this one. As you did before with RunDetailRowController, you could create a new file for this class. Personally, I prefer keeping all of these related classes in one file, but others disagree—the choice is yours. The class itself is easy, setting only two values to configure for a row:

Chapter 6/TapALap/TapALap WatchKit Extension/RunDetailsInterfaceController.swift

```
class LapDetailRowController: NSObject {

    @IBOutlet weak var lapNumberLabel: WKInterfaceLabel!
    @IBOutlet weak var lapDurationLabel: WKInterfaceLabel!

    lazy var durationFormatter: NSDateComponentsFormatter = {
        let durationFormatter = NSDateComponentsFormatter()
        durationFormatter.unitsStyle = .Positional
        return durationFormatter
    }()

    func configureForLap(lap: NSTimeInterval, atIndex index: UInt) {
        lapDurationLabel.setText(durationFormatter.stringFromTimeInterval(lap))
        lapNumberLabel.setText("\(index + 1)")
    }

}
```

Back in the storyboard, select the row controller you created. Change the class of the row controller to your new LapDetailRowController class, and then change its identifier to "LapRow." While you're there, be sure to connect the two @IBOutlet properties to their respective interface objects in the storyboard. Your UI is now finished. It should look like the image shown here:

When you want to display a run in this interface controller, you set the labels' values appropriately and then display the laps in the table. Implement this as a new method, configureForRun():

Chapter 6/TapALap/TapALap WatchKit Extension/RunDetailsInterfaceController.swift

```
func configureForRun(run: Run) {
    runDateLabel.setText(dateFormatter.stringFromDate(run.startDate))

    let lengthFormatter = NSLengthFormatter()
    runDistanceLabel.setText(lengthFormatter.stringFromMeters(run.distance))

    lapsTable.setNumberOfRows(run.laps.count, withRowType: "LapRow")
```

```
    for i in 0 ..< lapsTable.numberOfRows {
        if let rowController = lapsTable.rowControllerAtIndex(i) as?
            LapDetailRowController {
                let lapTime: NSTimeInterval = run.laps[i]
                rowController.configureForLap(lapTime, atIndex: UInt(i))
        }
    }

    let paceFormatter = NSDateComponentsFormatter()
    runPaceLabel.setText(paceFormatter.stringFromTimeInterval(run.pace))
}
```

Next, you need the dateFormatter property:

Chapter 6/TapALap/TapALap WatchKit Extension/RunDetailsInterfaceController.swift

```
lazy var dateFormatter: NSDateFormatter = {
    let dateFormatter = NSDateFormatter()
    dateFormatter.dateStyle = .MediumStyle
    dateFormatter.timeStyle = .NoStyle
    return dateFormatter
}()
```

You used a property of Run that doesn't exist yet: pace. Open Run.swift and add
it as a computed property:

Chapter 6/TapALap/TapALap WatchKit Extension/Run.swift

```
var pace: NSTimeInterval {
    return duration / NSTimeInterval(laps.count)
}
```

Handle the Run object that was passed in as context to awakeWithContext():

Chapter 6/TapALap/TapALap WatchKit Extension/RunDetailsInterfaceController.swift

```
override func awakeWithContext(context: AnyObject?) {
    super.awakeWithContext(context)

    if let run = context as? Run {
        configureForRun(run)
    }
}
```

And you're all set. Build and run the app, and you'll be
able to see the Run Details screen filled in with details,
just like in the image shown here:

As you can see, passing around context objects is pretty
easy. This is a great example of WatchKit learning from
UIKit's experience; whereas you would need to create
custom UIViewController subclasses with initializers (or
public properties) to take model objects, WatchKit has a

built-in method for passing data to interface controllers. Next, let's look at passing data back *from* an interface controller using a protocol.

Configuring Tracks in TapALap

Before you can actually go for a run in TapALap, you need a way to create a track. You'll allow your users to specify a name for the track, as well as how long a lap is. Once the track is complete, you'll need to send it back to the Go Running interface controller, and for that, you'll create a protocol. First, let's get the interface created for creating tracks.

The main screen you need to deal with is the track configuration screen. You'll use it to name a track as well as configure how long a lap on it is. You already have a class, TrackConfigurationInterfaceController, as well as an interface controller in your storyboard, for this task, so let's get started. To configure how long a track is, you're going to use a new user interface to this app: WKInterfacePicker. Given that most tracks express their distance in terms of how many laps make one mile (or appropriate local unit of distance), you'll ask the user to input how many laps add up to a distance that they also specify. This two-picker approach will allow for odd track configurations, like my local gym, in which seven laps adds up to one mile. For now we'll assume miles, but in a later chapter on page 177 you'll learn more about making apps work for users in all countries.

Creating the Track Configuration Interface

Open Interface.storyboard in Xcode and find the empty track configuration interface controller. First, you'll add a button to it that you'll use for setting the track's name. Since the track doesn't yet have a name, you'll set the title of the button to something instructive: "Tap to Set Name." Next, add a picker, a label, and then another picker. Set the text of the label to "equals" and then add all three items to a horizontal group. You don't want everything to be the same size, so set the width of the first picker to 0.25 relative to its container, the width of the label to 0.3, and the width of the second picker to 0.45. Set the height of the two pickers to 44 and the vertical alignment of the label to Center, and this group is done. For the pickers, there are some additional properties to set. Since you have two of them onscreen at once, you'll need to know which one has focus—that is, which one will move when the user moves the Digital Crown. In Xcode's Attributes Inspector, set the Indicator style of both to Shown While Focused. Then, set the Focus style of the first picker to Outline with Caption and the second to Outline. You'll read more about the caption later.

Finally, you'll need a button that saves the track. Add a button at the bottom with the title "Save." When this is done, you should have an interface controller laid out like so:

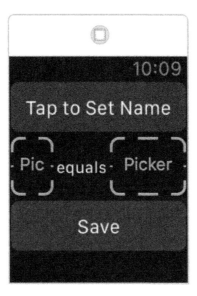

With your user interface laid out, you can create outlets for your interface objects in the interface controller class. Open TrackConfigurationInterfaceController.swift in Xcode and add outlets and actions for everything you'll need:

Chapter 6/TapALap/TapALap WatchKit Extension/TrackConfigurationInterfaceController.swift

```
@IBOutlet var nameButton: WKInterfaceButton!
@IBOutlet var lapsPicker: WKInterfacePicker!
@IBOutlet var distancePicker: WKInterfacePicker!

@IBAction func nameButtonPressed() {
}
@IBAction func lapsPickerDidChange(selectedIndex i: Int) {
}
@IBAction func distancePickerDidChange(selectedIndex i: Int) {
}
@IBAction func saveButtonPressed() {
}
```

Return to the storyboard and connect the outlets: nameButton to the top button, lapsPicker to the first picker, which you'll use to set the number of laps, and distancePicker to the second picker, which you'll use to set the total distance. Connect the name button to the nameButtonPressed() method and the save button to the saveButtonPressed() method. Next, you need to connect the pickers to their action methods. Whenever the user adjusts the picker, the method will be called with the index of the picker item the user has selected (more on picker items later). Because you've given the index the external parameter name selectedIndex, this will look a little different in Interface Builder. Since Interface Builder uses the Objective-C versions of the methods, it uses the Swift-to-Objective-C-translated name of the method, so connect the laps picker to the one called lapsPickerDidChangeWithSelectedIndex: and the distance picker to the one called distancePickerDidChangeWithSelectedIndex:. These names are automatically generated from your Swift code, even though you didn't type "With" anywhere.

With your outlets connected, but before you implement anything, let's think about when this screen is going to show up. When the user first starts TapALap, he won't have any tracks configured, so he'll tap the Selected Track button on the Go Running interface controller. Ideally, this button will take him to a screen where he can select from a list of saved tracks, but since he won't have any, you can jump straight to adding a new one. Let's set that up now and come back to this screen when you need it.

Displaying the Track Configuration Interface

Open GoRunningInterfaceController.swift. You haven't done much with this screen, so let's add some additional functionality. First, you need a way to save the currently selected track, so you'll add an optional variable for it:

Chapter 6/TapALap/TapALap WatchKit Extension/GoRunningInterfaceController.swift

```
var selectedTrack: Track?
```

If the user has yet to select a track, you'll need to tell him that he needs to select a track, so you'll modify the startRunButtonPressed() method to ensure that one is selected. First, however, you need to modify the declaration of Track itself, changing it from a struct to a class. Open Track.swift and make the change (aside from changing "struct" to "class," you'll need to add an initializer, since only structs get initializers created for free):

Chapter 6/TapALap/TapALap WatchKit Extension/Track.swift

```
class Track {
    let name: String
    let lapDistance: Double // in meters

    init(name: String, lapDistance: Double) {
        self.name = name
        self.lapDistance = lapDistance
    }
}
```

Now that you've changed Track to a class, you can implement your startRunButtonPressed() to ensure that the user has selected one:

Chapter 6/TapALap/TapALap WatchKit Extension/GoRunningInterfaceController.swift

```
@IBAction func startRunButtonPressed() {
    guard let track = selectedTrack else {
        presentAlertControllerWithTitle("Error",
            message: "You need to select a track to run on!",
            preferredStyle: .Alert,
            actions: [
                WKAlertAction(title: "OK",
                    style: .Default,
                    handler: {})
            ])

        return
    }

    let names = ["RunTimer"]

    WKInterfaceController.reloadRootControllersWithNames(names,
        contexts: [track])
}
```

To do this, you use a simple guard statement. If the user has *not* selected a track, then you'll use an *alert controller* to display an error message to him. The OK button of the alert controller is represented by a WKAlertAction instance, and you give it an empty closure for its handler since you don't need to do anything when the user taps it—the alert controller is automatically dismissed. At the end of the method, instead of passing nil as the context to the Run Timer interface controller, you'll pass the selected track. This is why you needed to make Track a class; since the type of the contexts array is [AnyObject], you can use only classes with it. You'll see passing context objects again later in this chapter. Now, if the user tries to start a run without selecting a track, he'll see this alert controller:

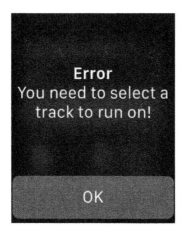

Next, you need to make the track name and lap distance labels display accurate data for the selected track. You haven't made outlets for them yet, so do that now:

Chapter 6/TapALap/TapALap WatchKit Extension/GoRunningInterfaceController.swift

```
@IBOutlet weak var trackNameLabel: WKInterfaceLabel!
@IBOutlet weak var trackDistanceLabel: WKInterfaceLabel!
```

Open the storyboard and connect the labels to those outlets. Next, you'll need to fill them in with data. Open GoRunningInterfaceController.swift again and add a updateTrackLabels() method, as well as an NSLengthFormatter:

Chapter 6/TapALap/TapALap WatchKit Extension/GoRunningInterfaceController.swift

```
lazy var distanceFormatter = NSLengthFormatter()

func updateTrackLabels() {
    if let track = selectedTrack {
        trackNameLabel.setText(track.name)

        trackDistanceLabel.setText(
            distanceFormatter.stringFromMeters(track.lapDistance))
    }
    else {
        trackNameLabel.setText("None")
        trackDistanceLabel.setText(nil)
    }
}
```

When you call this method, it'll update your labels, whether or not you have a track selected. You'll call it whenever the interface controller is about to appear to ensure that you always have the correct data onscreen:

Chapter 6/TapALap/TapALap WatchKit Extension/GoRunningInterfaceController.swift

```
override func willActivate() {
    super.willActivate()

    updateTrackLabels()
}
```

Now that you've added this method, if you build and run the app, you'll see None under Selected Track, instead of the canned data you added in the storyboard:

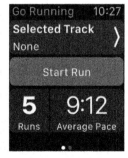

This screen is looking good! When the user starts your app and tries to start a run, he's prompted to create a track. When he taps to select a track, the track configuration screen appears, with the UI you created. Next, you need to tackle what happens when the user configures his track—you'll need to come back to this screen with a track. To that end, let's set up a new protocol for track selection. In Objective-C, you might be tempted to name a protocol something like TrackSelectionDelegate, but in Swift, the name should really involve what the type *does*. Name it TrackSelectionReceiver, to indicate that a type that conforms to it *receives* the track.

Creating the **TrackSelectionReceiver** Protocol

Open TrackConfigurationInterfaceController.swift and add the protocol declaration. You'll need just one method, receiveTrack(_:):

Chapter 6/TapALap/TapALap WatchKit Extension/TrackConfigurationInterfaceController.swift

```
protocol TrackSelectionReceiver: class {
    func receiveTrack(track: Track)
}
```

You mark the protocol as class so that it applies only to classes—later, you'll need to use some class-specific behavior in WatchKit. With this protocol, you'll be able to send the track from the track configuration screen to the Go Running screen. Let's set up the relationship between the screens now. Add a new property to TrackConfigurationInterfaceController called trackReceiver:

Chapter 6/TapALap/TapALap WatchKit Extension/TrackConfigurationInterfaceController.swift

```
weak var trackReceiver: TrackSelectionReceiver?
```

To set this variable, you'll implement awakeWithContext(_:) and try to convert the context parameter to a TrackSelectionReceiver:

Chapter 6/TapALap/TapALap WatchKit Extension/TrackConfigurationInterfaceController.swift

```
override func awakeWithContext(context: AnyObject?) {
    super.awakeWithContext(context)

    if let receiver = context as? TrackSelectionReceiver {
        self.trackReceiver = receiver
    }
}
```

Now, when you have a track, you'll just call receiveTrack(_:) on the trackReceiver to return to the previous screen. Let's implement that in GoRunningInterfaceController.swift by declaring that the class conforms to the TrackReceiver protocol and implementing the method:

```swift
class GoRunningInterfaceController: WKInterfaceController, TrackSelectionReceiver {

    func receiveTrack(track: Track) {
        selectedTrack = track
        updateTrackLabels()
        dismissController()
    }

    // The rest of the class follows…
```

This method will use the track you supplied, as well as dismiss the track configuration interface controller. Before it's called, however, you'll need to create an actual Track to send it.

Creating a Track

To create a track, you need to know two things: its name and how long one lap is. You've created outlets for all of your UIs, so let's write the code to get that data from your UI and save it as a Track. You'll start with the track's name. When the user taps the name button, you'll use WatchKit's *text input controller* to allow him to enter a name. Since there's no keyboard on the watch, you'll prepopulate the text input with some suggested names, as well as allow the user to dictate his response. Still in TrackConfigurationInterfaceController.swift, let's implement nameButtonPressed() to do this:

```swift
var selectedName: String?

@IBAction func nameButtonPressed() {
    let suggestedTrackNames = ["Gym", "School", "Park", "Trail", "Neighborhood"]

    presentTextInputControllerWithSuggestions(suggestedTrackNames,
        allowedInputMode: .Plain) { results in
            guard let name = results?.first as? String else { return }

            self.nameButton.setTitle(name)

            self.selectedName = name
    }
}
```

Start with our suggested track names, which you pass into presentTextInputControllerWithSuggestions(_:allowedInputMode:). Setting the allowed input mode to .Plain prevents the user from selecting emoji for a track name. The completion handler you pass in has one parameter, which you've named results. It's of type [AnyObject]?, so you need to make sure it contains a String you can use as a name. It could be nil if the user cancelled or contain an NSData object filled with image data if the user selected an emoji image. Assuming you have a name, set it as the title of your name button. Save it as selectedName, a property added here so you can reference the name later. Build and run, and you can see the text entry yourself. Tap the microphone to open the dictation window:

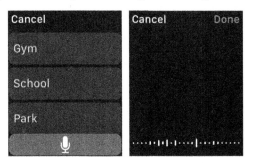

Once the user has selected or dictated a name, you return to the configuration screen. Next, you need to handle the track length selection. Before you can handle the user selecting picker items to choose the track length, you need to add those items to the pickers. You'll do that in awakeWithContext(_:):

Chapter 6/TapALap/TapALap WatchKit Extension/TrackConfigurationInterfaceController.swift

```
override func awakeWithContext(context: AnyObject?) {
    super.awakeWithContext(context)

    if let receiver = context as? TrackSelectionReceiver {
        self.trackReceiver = receiver
    }

    // Add 1-10 laps for laps picker
    let lapItems: [WKPickerItem] = (1 ... 10).map { i in
        let pickerItem = WKPickerItem()
        pickerItem.title = "\(i)"
        pickerItem.caption = (i == 1) ? "Lap" : "Laps"
        return pickerItem
    }

    lapsPicker.setItems(lapItems)

    // Add 0.5 - 5 miles for total distance picker
    var distanceItems: [WKPickerItem] = []

    let distanceFormatter = NSLengthFormatter()
    distanceFormatter.numberFormatter.minimumFractionDigits = 1
    distanceFormatter.numberFormatter.maximumFractionDigits = 1

    for i in 0.5.stride(to: 5.5, by:0.5) {
        let pickerItem = WKPickerItem()
        pickerItem.title = distanceFormatter.stringFromValue(i,
            unit: .Mile)
```

```
30          distanceItems.append(pickerItem)
        }

        distancePicker.setItems(distanceItems)

35      // Set values based on initial picker values.
        lapsPickerDidChange(selectedIndex: 0)
        distancePickerDidChange(selectedIndex: 0)
    }
```

The pickers are initialized with WKPickerItem instances. You start on line 9 by creating an array of them with their title property set to the numbers 1 to 10. The title is displayed inside the picker as the user scrolls the Digital Crown. The caption is displayed in a green bubble outside the picker and describes the thing the user is selecting. You set it to "Lap" or "Laps" to inform the user that here he's selecting the number of laps. With this array in place, you call setItems(_:) on the picker on line 16 to send the values to the picker for selection.

You handle the distance selection similarly, but you use the stride(to:by:) method on line 25 to generate values from 0.5 miles to 5.0 miles, with a value at every 0.5-mile mark. With an NSLengthFormatter, you set the title appropriately and then finally call setItems(_:) on your distance picker. You don't set the caption variable here because the title includes the unit of measure, so it should be pretty clear to the user what he's setting. Finally, you call your callback methods, lapsPickerDidChange(selectedIndex:) and distancePickerDidChange(selectedIndex:), with your initial values. Unlike pickers on iOS, pickers on watchOS start with the first item selected, so you call these callbacks to set your initial state.

Whenever the user adjusts the values in the pickers, you'll receive the callbacks again with the index of the selected item. Let's implement those now:

Chapter 6/TapALap/TapALap WatchKit Extension/TrackConfigurationInterfaceController.swift

```
var selectedLaps: Int?
var selectedDistance: Double?

@IBAction func lapsPickerDidChange(selectedIndex i: Int) {
    selectedLaps = i + 1
}

@IBAction func distancePickerDidChange(selectedIndex i: Int) {
    // Convert from miles to meters
    selectedDistance = Double(i + 1) / 2.0 * 1609.34
}
```

First, you create some storage for the selected values: selectedLaps and selected-Distance. Then, in each method, you use the i parameter to get the actual selected value. For laps, you can simply add one: the value at index 0 is 1 lap. For distance, you convert the selected distance (in miles) to meters for storage. With all of your values now saved, you can finally create a Track when the user taps the Save button:

Chapter 6/TapALap/TapALap WatchKit Extension/TrackConfigurationInterfaceController.swift

```
@IBAction func saveButtonPressed() {
    guard let name = selectedName else {
        presentAlertControllerWithTitle("Error",
            message: "You must select a name for your track.",
            preferredStyle: .Alert,
            actions: [
                WKAlertAction(title: "OK",
                    style: .Default,
                    handler: {})
            ])

        return
    }

    guard let laps = selectedLaps, distance = selectedDistance else {
        fatalError("No laps/distance selected. Double-check your implementation"
            + " of awakeWithContext(_:)!")
    }

    let lapDistance = distance / Double(laps)

    let track = Track(name: name, lapDistance: lapDistance)

    trackReceiver?.receiveTrack(track)
}
```

In this method, you ensure that you have a name, a number of laps, and a distance, showing an alert to the user if he hasn't selected a name. Since you called your picker callbacks in awakeWithContext(_:), you should already have values for the number of laps and the distance; if you don't, you'll call fatalError() and crash, because something has obviously gone wrong.

In possession of a name, the number of laps, and the distance of those laps, you can now create a Track. Once you do, you can pass it to the track receiver, which will handle dismissing this interface controller and using the track for your run.

Wrap-Up

Your app is pretty navigable now. You can get from point A to point B reliably, and your data is flowing around nicely from interface controller to interface controller. In the next chapter, we'll look at the WatchKit extension as a whole, examining its lifecycle and applying it to real-world scenarios with your app.

WatchKit Extension Lifecycle

By now your watch app is pretty sophisticated. You're moving between screens, sending data back and forth, and even replacing your entire UI as needed. But what about all of the *other* code you want to write—running code when the app starts, handling OS events, and the like? On iOS, you'd use your app delegate to handle the app's lifecycle methods that run when the user starts or leaves the app. The equivalent on watchOS is the *extension delegate*, a class you'll implement to handle the lifecycle events of your watch app. TapALap already has an extension delegate; it was created automatically by Xcode when we created the project, but it doesn't do anything. In this chapter, you'll implement TapALap's extension delegate, allowing the app to safely continue a run if it's suspended during one. We'll also look at receiving notifications in the extension delegate, a common task for many apps, and look at Handoff, which allows an app to continue a user's activity from one device to another. First, let's add some lifecycle methods to TapALap.

Adding Lifecycle Methods

The lifecycle methods of WKExtensionDelegate and UIApplication (on iOS) protocols are similar, though they are fewer. The most common one to implement is applicationDidFinishLaunching(), allowing you to do setup when the app is launched. The other two have you covered when the app is interrupted—for example, if the user gets a call in the middle of a run. First, applicationWillResignActive() will be called on your delegate, allowing you to save your work, and then applicationDidBecomeActive() lets you restore it once the app is back in the foreground.

The WatchKit extension lifecycle methods are shown here in the context of launching a WatchKit app. You see the state of the app from before it's launched to when it's running and all of the methods watchOS calls on its extension delegate in the process in the figure on page 84.

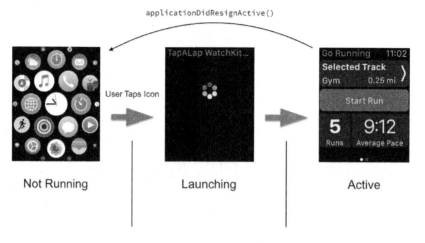

applicationDidResignActive()

Not Running   Launching   Active

applicationDidFinishLaunching()   applicationDidBecomeActive()

The first of these methods, applicationDidFinishLaunching(), serves a very important role in WatchKit: it allows you to control the interface controller that the user is presented with when she starts the app. If you do nothing, then watchOS will load your storyboard and present whichever interface controller is marked as the initial interface controller. That isn't always what you want, however. If, for instance, your user is already running but the app stops—perhaps it crashed (however unlikely) or the user went to do something with the music app that caused watchOS to suspend TapALap—then you wouldn't want to start that user back at the Go Running screen. Instead, you'd want her to be taken directly to the run timer so she can continue her run. Ideally, all of her data will still be present and she'll be able to continue the run. In fact, the user may not even notice that the app has restarted! Your goal should be to make the app launch seamlessly, regardless of how the user left it.

To facilitate this experience, you're going to need to save the run data as you go. A great time to do that is when you mark the start date and begin timing the run. Before you write the code, however, let's consider your options for saving the data. You could use HealthKit, but that would be a lot of code for your first version of the app. (We'll cover using HealthKit in a later chapter on page 151.) You could create an SQLite database, but you really only need to save a few pieces of data. For cases like this, just like on iOS, NSUserDefaults can be a great way to store small key-value pairs of data. You'll use that, saving your run's startDate and lapTimes values to it. You'll do this in RunTimerInterfaceController.swift, so let's head there and get to work! Let's do some refactoring to willActivate() to handle the case where a run has already been started:

```swift
override func willActivate() {
    super.willActivate()

    if lapTimes == nil || startDate == nil {
        let userDefaults = NSUserDefaults.standardUserDefaults()

        if let date = userDefaults.objectForKey("StartDate") as? NSDate,
            times = userDefaults.objectForKey("LapTimes") as? [NSTimeInterval] {
                startDate = date
                lapTimes = times
        }
        else {
            startRun()
        }
    }

    updateDistanceLabel()
}

func startRun() {
    lapTimes = []
    startDate = NSDate()

    let userDefaults = NSUserDefaults.standardUserDefaults()
    userDefaults.setObject(startDate, forKey: "StartDate")
    userDefaults.setObject(lapTimes, forKey: "LapTimes")
    userDefaults.synchronize()
}
```

When this code runs, if the interface controller doesn't have an existing run, it'll first look to see if there's one stored in the user defaults. If not, then it'll call startRun() to create one. Next, you'll need to update the saved lapTimes array in the user defaults at the end of every lap:

```swift
@IBAction func finishLapButtonPressed() {
    let lapFinishTime = NSDate()

    guard let startDate = startDate, lapTimes = lapTimes else { return }

    let totalRunDuration = lapFinishTime.timeIntervalSinceDate(startDate)

    let cumulativeLapDuration = lapTimes.reduce(0, combine: { $0 + $1 })

    let lapDuration = totalRunDuration - cumulativeLapDuration

    self.lapTimes?.append(lapDuration)

    updateDistanceLabel()

    let userDefaults = NSUserDefaults.standardUserDefaults()
    userDefaults.setObject(lapTimes, forKey: "LapTimes")
    userDefaults.synchronize()
}
```

There you have it. Your run will now resume automatically when returning to the run timer. To see this in action, force-quit the app during a run, and then restart it and tap Start Run again; this will open the run timer and display your still-in-progress run. You're halfway there; next, let's tell the app to open directly to the run timer when starting if there's a run started.

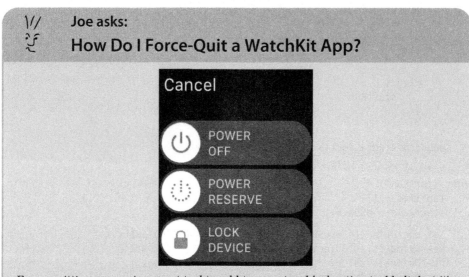

Joe asks:

How Do I Force-Quit a WatchKit App?

Force-quitting an app is a great tool to add to your troubleshooting tool belt, but it's not the most discoverable process. When the app is running, hold down the side button on your Apple Watch (not the Digital Crown but the button next to it) until the screen with the Power Off button appears, as you see here. Release the button; then press and hold the same button again. You'll see the app animate away; it's now been force-quit.

Open ExtensionDelegate.swift in the WatchKit extension and add some code to applicationDidFinishLaunching() to handle runs in progress:

Chapter 7/TapALap/TapALap WatchKit Extension/ExtensionDelegate.swift

```
func applicationDidFinishLaunching() {
    returnToInProgressRun()
}

func returnToInProgressRun() {
    let userDefaults = NSUserDefaults.standardUserDefaults()

    if let _ = userDefaults.objectForKey("LapTimes") as? [NSTimeInterval],
        _ = userDefaults.objectForKey("StartDate") as? NSDate {
            WKInterfaceController.reloadRootControllersWithNames(
                ["RunTimer"], contexts: nil)
    }
}
```

As you can see, you don't need the values of the start date or lap times here, so you use the underscore to discard their values. It's only important to this code that the values exist as the correct types. Build and run the app, and you'll see that if there's a run started, the app opens *directly* to the run timer, without ever loading the Go Running interface controller. Perfect!

If you tap Finish Run and then restart the app, you'll see what you need to do next: clear out the data when a run is finished. This is a pretty simple addition to the endRun() method of RunTimerInterfaceController:

Chapter 7/TapALap/TapALap WatchKit Extension/RunTimerInterfaceController.swift

```swift
func endRun() {
    let names = ["GoRunning", "RunLog"]

    let contexts: [AnyObject]?

    if let lapTimes = lapTimes, startDate = startDate {
        let distance = track.lapDistance * Double(lapTimes.count)

        let run = Run(distance: distance,
            laps: lapTimes,
            startDate: startDate)

        let userDefaults = NSUserDefaults.standardUserDefaults()
        userDefaults.removeObjectForKey("LapTimes")
        userDefaults.removeObjectForKey("StartDate")
        userDefaults.synchronize()

        contexts = [NSNull(), run]
    }
    else {
        contexts = nil
    }

    WKInterfaceController.reloadRootControllersWithNames(names,
        contexts: contexts)
}
```

Now that you're deleting these values once you've created a Run instance out of them, the app will only reopen to a run before it's finished. Try it out!

As you've seen, the lifecycle methods of WKExtensionDelegate allow you to customize your app's behavior at launch and other important times when your interface controllers' code alone wouldn't be enough for a seamless user experience. They also allow you some more control over the coupling in your app; your interface code can stay in interface controllers, while your extension lifecycle code has its own place to exist. The extension delegate is good for more than lifecycle methods, however. Next, let's look at some system APIs you can integrate with in your extension delegate.

Adopting Handoff in the Extension Delegate

Handoff is a technology permeating many Apple platforms: iOS, OS X, and watchOS. It relies on the concept of a *user activity*, which describes the *thing* that the user is doing. This could be editing a document, ordering a pizza, or playing a game. On iOS and OS X, adopting Handoff and user activities allows you to transfer that activity from one device to another. You can seamlessly edit a document on one device and then open the same app on another device right to the same document. On watchOS, Handoff has two main purposes: to continue an action on the user's iPhone, just as you can among other Apple devices, and to navigate into the watch app from other user interfaces, such as the app's Glance. A simple calculator app on watchOS, for instance, could use Handoff to open its counterpart on iOS where more advanced calculator features are possible. For a Glance, using Handoff inside the app helps you to open the app right to the relevant portion covered by the Glance. For example, an airline watch app's glance might show you your next flight details, while the watch app might open to your profile screen with frequent flier points and such; using Handoff from the Glance, you'd open the watch app right to the next flight details.

Unlike iOS, where you'd create an NSUserActivity instance yourself and mark it as the current activity, watchOS relies on your interface controller to provide activity data indirectly using the updateUserActivity(_:userInfo:webpageURL:) method. The three arguments you provide give your other devices information about how to handle the user activity: an identifier for the activity, such as "com.pragprog.readingabook," an optional userInfo dictionary to pass more information about it, and an optional webpageURL parameter to open a website on a device without an app that can handle the activity. Using this method in WatchKit interface controllers automatically sets up Handoff for properly configured apps, but that's not all it can do.

In an app's Glance, you can't add interactivity of any kind. No buttons, pickers, or anything of that sort. So what happens when the user taps a Glance? The answer lies in Handoff. watchOS piggybacks on the Handoff system to open apps directly to specific points. For instance, if you have a Glance relating to a specific part of the app, the extension delegate can handle the user's tap and navigate to the correct area of the app. First, implement updateUserActivity(_:userInfo:webpageURL:) inside the glance, including some information about the user's activity in the userInfo parameter. Then in the extension delegate, implement handleUserActivity(_:). In this method, parse the userInfo to determine the appropriate course of action. Just as you returned to the run timer in

TapALap if the app was launched while a run was in progress, this method is the perfect time to switch the app's UI to the appropriate screen.

Although watchOS doesn't have any hooks for using Handoff to launch apps from other devices, there's one more way to use Handoff: to launch an app from the watch face. You'll learn more about that when you learn about complications later in this book on page 113.

Responding to Notifications

The extension delegate also handles local and remote notifications for watchOS apps. The methods to implement in the protocol mirror those for responding to notifications on iOS and for good reason—one of the primary use cases of the Apple Watch is to act as a conduit for iOS app notifications—whether or not the app has an Apple Watch–specific app. When the user's iPhone is locked and the Apple Watch is unlocked, all notifications are routed to the watch by default. The real power of notifications on the watch comes with *actions* associated with these notifications; as you can see in this screenshot, a notification can include buttons that perform actions when the user selects them. When a notification comes in, you use the extension delegate to handle the user's interaction with it on the watch.

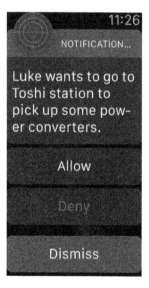

The four methods available for handling notifications that come in when your app isn't running are all very similar. For instance, handleActionWithIdentifier(_:forRemoteNotification:withResponseInfo:) is called for remote notifications that include an optional text reply. The first parameter is a string identifier for the notification button the user tapped—something like Accept for a calendar invitation. The remoteNotification parameter contains the notification information from the remote server, and the responseInfo parameter can optionally contain text from the user—such as a reply to a text message. The other three methods like this one are simple variations on a theme: exchange "Local" for "Remote" when dealing with local notifications, and omit the "withResponseInfo:" portion for notifications without extra info. When implementing these methods, you simply perform the action the user selected, using the text entered if needed. Handling notifications this way is a great tool to allow users to do things quickly.

Of course, the user may be using the app when a notification comes in. Perhaps your app allows the user to start a potentially long-running task, like preheating an oven, and the server sends a push notification when it's done. If the user is currently using the app, the extension delegate's didReceiveRemoteNotification(_:) method is called, with a userInfo dictionary containing the notification payload. There's a corresponding local notification version as well. In this method, it's best to present the user with the information from the notification—or at least update the app's UI.

There may not be much to notifications in watchOS, but they're incredibly useful on the device. Since it's always with the user, the watch is the perfect device to make quick decisions on notifications. Enabling users to perform quick tasks with the tap of a button on their wrist can save them valuable time and make your app indispensable in their workflow.

Wrap-Up

As you can see, the WatchKit extension delegate performs many of the same tasks as an app delegate on iOS. The API is a bit pared down to coincide with the more streamlined feature set of watchOS, but through a few simple pieces of implementation, a well-designed extension delegate can make the difference between an average Apple Watch app and an exquisite one. You've seen how to take advantage of the extension's lifecycle to ensure a seamless UI experience for your app, how to use Handoff to open your app right to the information a user was looking at in your Glance, and how to use notifications to allow users to perform actions at the raise of a wrist. Next, let's look at how your code can reach outside the extension and communicate with other devices, using external networks to open a fountain of data possibilities.

CHAPTER 8

Communicating with WatchConnectivity

At some point in an app's development lifecycle, the device itself is not enough. We can do a lot of cool and interesting things on the watch, but eventually we need the app to communicate with the outside world. Whether it's making a network request to fetch remote data or communicating with the companion iPhone app to fetch data from our users' pockets, we need a way to get data into our apps. Luckily, getting remote data is very straightforward on Apple Watch. In this chapter, we'll cover the two ways you'll be getting data into your apps: direct network requests, where the watch app communicates directly with a server, and using the *WatchConnectivity* framework to communicate with the user's iPhone. Let's start with direct network requests.

Making Network Requests on Apple Watch

Fortunately, networking on watchOS is incredibly easy. In traditional Apple fashion, "it just works." We can use the NSURLSession class to make network requests, download files in the background, and upload files. If you want to use a third-party networking library, such as AFNetworking or Alamofire, you can use them just as on iOS, so long as they use NSURLSession and not its predecessor, NSURLConnection.[1] One thing that's transparent to us as watchOS app developers is the actual device used to perform network requests. If the watch's paired iPhone is connected, NSURLSession connections will use the iPhone as a proxy. Otherwise, the watch will connect to known Wi-Fi networks and perform the request itself. By leaving the network routing behavior as an implementation detail, the watch can do whatever is best for performance and battery life. As developers, we just need to use the same code as on iOS to connect

---

1.   For more information about networking on watchOS and iOS, read Apple's URL Loading System Programming Guide at https://developer.apple.com/library/watchos/documentation/Cocoa/Conceptual/URLLoadingSystem.

to servers, and it works. We won't do a full sample project for this, since most projects will have more in-depth networking, with libraries and frameworks, but here's a simple URL connection for watchOS:

```
guard let url = NSURL(string: "https://www.example.com") else { return }

let request = NSURLRequest(URL: url)

NSURLSession.sharedSession().dataTaskWithRequest(request) { (data: NSData?,
  response: NSURLResponse?, error: NSError?) -> Void in
    guard let data = data,
        html = String(data: data,
          encoding: NSUTF8StringEncoding) else { return }

  print("Received HTML: \(html)")
}.resume()
```

In this example, making a network request is simple. First, we make an NSURL instance from a string, bailing early if this fails. Then, we create an NSURLRequest for this URL. If we needed to do additional work on the request, such as adding HTTP headers, we'd do it here. Next, we create a new data task on the shared NSURLSession, passing in the request and a completion handler. The completion handler, having received data from the server as an NSData instance, turns it into a String and prints it. Finally, we call resume() on the data task to start it. Just like that, we're getting data back from a remote server—on our watch! Now that you've seen how to get network connections up and running, let's look at using WatchConnectivity to communicate with the iPhone.

Preparing for WatchConnectivity: Persisting Data in TapALap

One of the more confusing parts of TapALap is the track selection and configuration process, which makes it an ideal candidate for the iPhone instead. The user should be able to do everything he needs before he runs on the watch, since he might install the app and leave his phone behind—for instance, in a gym locker room—but there are some things you can leave to the user's iPhone instead: renaming tracks, editing lap distance, or deleting tracks. You'll use the WatchConnectivity framework to synchronize your track data from watchOS to iOS and use the iPhone app for more advanced editing. Before you can get into WatchConnectivity, you'll need to add a way to persist track data in TapALap so that your tracks last for more than one run.

Persisting Track Data

Once again, you're faced with the question of how to store your data. Since you're going to have a small amount of data—most users won't have hundreds of tracks configured—you can use the user defaults system as a generic key-value store and save your tracks there. Open up Track.swift and add a method to save tracks to disk. You can't save them directly to NSUserDefaults, so instead create a dictionaryRepresentation() method to convert them to a Dictionary and then an init(dictionaryRepresentation:) method to create a Track from the saved dictionary:

Chapter 8/TapALap/TapALap WatchKit Extension/Track.swift

```swift
func dictionaryRepresentation() -> [String: AnyObject] {
    return ["Name": name, "LapDistance": lapDistance]
}

init?(dictionaryRepresentation dictionary: [String: AnyObject]) {
    guard let name = dictionary["Name"] as? String,
        lapDistance = dictionary["LapDistance"] as? Double
        else {
            return nil
    }

    self.name = name
    self.lapDistance = lapDistance
}
```

With this code in place, you can now convert your Track objects to dictionaries and save them in NSUserDefaults, as well as load them back:

Chapter 8/TapALap/TapALap WatchKit Extension/Track.swift

```swift
static func savedTracks() -> [Track] {
    guard let trackDictionaries = NSUserDefaults.standardUserDefaults()
        .objectForKey("SavedTracks") as? [[String: AnyObject]]
        else { return [] }

    return trackDictionaries.flatMap(Track.init)
}

func save() {
    var tracks = Track.savedTracks()

    guard !tracks.contains(self) else { return }

    tracks.append(self)

    let trackDictionaries: [[String: AnyObject]] = tracks.map {
        $0.dictionaryRepresentation()
    }

    do {
        let newContext = ["Tracks": trackDictionaries]

        try WCSession.defaultSession().updateApplicationContext(newContext)
    }
    catch let error {
        NSLog("Error saving tracks to application context: \(error).")
    }
```

```
NSUserDefaults.standardUserDefaults().setObject(trackDictionaries,
    forKey: "SavedTracks")
}
```

In these methods, you use map() and flatMap() to painlessly convert between types. flatMap() is especially useful, because the init(dictionaryRepresentation:) method you wrote could return nil if the dictionary doesn't contain the right values; in that case, flatMap() simply discards the nil values and returns an array of Track objects that were successfully created. In save(), once you have an array of Dictionary objects representing your Tracks, you can use WatchConnectivity by calling the WCSession's updateApplicationContext(_:) method. This will send the dictionaries to the phone, where you'll access them later.

You need to make one more change for this to compile: before you can use contains(_:) on the existing array to see if the track is already saved, Track needs to conform to the Equatable protocol; to tell if the object already exists in the array, you need to know if it's the same as any object in the array. A Track is equal to another track if their names and lap distances match, so to conform to Equatable, all you need to do is implement ==(lhs:rhs:). Let's do that now:

Chapter 8/TapALap/TapALap WatchKit Extension/Track.swift

```
func ==(lhs: Track, rhs: Track) -> Bool {
    return lhs.name == rhs.name && lhs.lapDistance == rhs.lapDistance
}

extension Track: Equatable {}
```

Now you can support saving your tracks and reusing them. Next, let's make it possible for the user to switch between saved tracks when the app starts up. Open GoRunningInterfaceController.swift and make a couple of changes to support selecting between a list of tracks. Specifically, if you have saved tracks, you should show a list of tracks to choose from instead of the track configuration screen. You can make that change in trackButtonPressed():

Chapter 8/TapALap/TapALap WatchKit Extension/GoRunningInterfaceController.swift

```
@IBAction func trackButtonPressed() {
    if Track.savedTracks().isEmpty {
        presentControllerWithName("TrackConfiguration", context: self)
    }
    else {
        presentControllerWithName("TrackSelection", context: self)
    }
}
```

If the list of saved tracks is empty, you'll jump right to the track configuration interface. Otherwise, you'll display an interface controller with the identifier

TrackSelection, which will display a list of tracks to choose from. Let's create that interface controller next.

Choosing Between Saved Tracks

To choose between tracks, you'll need a new interface controller. Open Interface.storyboard and drag out a new interface controller, giving it the title "Tracks" and the identifier "TrackSelection." Add a table to it and then a button. In the table, add two labels, making the first use the Headline font style and the second use the Caption 2 font style, as well as aligned to the right. Give them the titles "Name" and "Distance," which is what they'll be used for. Give the button the title "Add New." This is the basic layout of the screen: each row represents a track, and the Add New button will create a new track. You can set up that segue now—Control-drag from the button to the track configuration screen and choose the modal segue type. Select the segue and give it the identifier "AddNewTrack" so you can reference it from code. With that, your UI is complete. It should look like the following image:

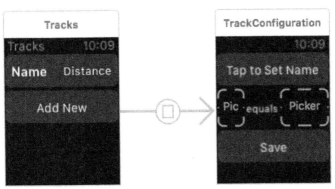

Now you need a class to put your code into. Create a new interface controller class and name it TrackSelectionInterfaceController. Before you write any code, connect your user interface so you don't forget. You'll need an outlet for the table and a row controller with outlets for the two labels you created:

Chapter 8/TapALap/TapALap WatchKit Extension/TrackSelectionInterfaceController.swift

```swift
class TrackRowController: NSObject {

    @IBOutlet weak var nameLabel: WKInterfaceLabel!
    @IBOutlet weak var distanceLabel: WKInterfaceLabel!

}

    // Inside of the TrackSelectionInterfaceController
    @IBOutlet weak var table: WKInterfaceTable!
```

Head back to the storyboard. You need to change the class of your new interface controller to TrackSelectionInterfaceController, change the class of the table row controller to TrackRowController, and connect your three outlets to the appropriate interface objects. You also need to give the row controller an identifier. Set it to "TrackRow" so you can create a row later. With your outlets connected, you can now put data into your table.

Populating the Track List Table

First, create a tracks computed property that returns the tracks you saved into NSUserDefaults but sorted by name. Then create a length formatter for use in the table. You actually load the data in loadTableData(), which you also call in willActivate() to ensure you always have an up-to-date list of tracks. Finally, loadTableData() creates a row controller for each track and configures the row with the track's name and lap distance. Pretty straightforward! Next, you'll implement what happens when the user taps a row.

Responding to Track Selection

When the user taps a table row, watchOS will call table(_:didSelectRowAtIndex:) on your interface controller. When that happens, you'll need to do something with the track. You can reuse the TrackSelectionReceiver protocol for this and send the track back to the Go Running interface controller the same way the track configuration page does:

Chapter 8/TapALap/TapALap WatchKit Extension/TrackSelectionInterfaceController.swift

```
weak var trackReceiver: TrackSelectionReceiver?

override func awakeWithContext(context: AnyObject?) {
    super.awakeWithContext(context)

    if let receiver = context as? TrackSelectionReceiver {
        self.trackReceiver = receiver
    }
}

override func table(table: WKInterfaceTable,
    didSelectRowAtIndex rowIndex: Int) {
        trackReceiver?.receiveTrack(tracks[rowIndex])
}
```

Just as you would on the track configuration screen, you define a trackReceiver property and attempt to set it in awakeWithContext(_:). When the user taps a row, you call receiveTrack(_:) on the receiver, which takes care of dismissing this screen. So far, so good! Next, you'll take care of the Add button.

Adding New Tracks

Not only will your TrackSelectionInterfaceController have a TrackSelectionReceiver to send selected tracks *to*, it will itself conform to the protocol to receive tracks *from* the track configuration screen. This way, when a user selects Add New Track and then creates a new track, you can handle the new track and pass it back to the Go Running interface controller:

Chapter 8/TapALap/TapALap WatchKit Extension/TrackSelectionInterfaceController.swift

```swift
class TrackSelectionInterfaceController: WKInterfaceController,
TrackSelectionReceiver {

    override func contextForSegueWithIdentifier(
        segueIdentifier: String) -> AnyObject? {
            if segueIdentifier == "AddNewTrack" {
                return self
            }

            return nil
    }

    func receiveTrack(track: Track) {
        dismissController()

        track.save()
        loadTableData()
        trackReceiver?.receiveTrack(track)

    }
}
```

Here, in contextForSegueWithIdentifier(_:), you pass self to register yourself as the receiver for the new track. When the user configures his new track, you'll get it in receiveTrack(_:) and then pass it back to the Go Running interface controller. The user will see both screens dismiss and his new track will be selected.

With these changes, you can now persist your track data across launches and have multiple tracks that you keep track of, and you're all set to go. But what if you want to rename a track, edit its lap distance, or even delete it altogether? For that, you'll use TapALap's as-yet-unused iPhone app, and you'll use WatchConnectivity to send the data back and forth.

Talking to the iPhone with WatchConnectivity

Talking to remote servers in a data center somewhere is an important task for any app, but sometimes on the watch it seems redundant. Why talk to a server on another continent when there's a perfectly good iPhone just a Bluetooth connection away? That's where the WatchConnectivity framework comes in. Often, we just want to send small bits of data back and forth between the two devices—preferences, small images, or user documents, for instance. WatchConnectivity serves as a bridge between the two apps—in fact, you'll use the framework on both iOS and watchOS. There are several ways to transfer data back and forth using WatchConnectivity. As we go through them, you'll implement TapALap's iPhone app to handle the more advanced features you want to include.

Creating a WCSession Communication Channel

To communicate with the watch app, the iOS app needs an object that implements the WCSessionDelegate protocol. This object will be responsible for all communication with the watch, so you'll want to create it as early as possible in your iPhone app's lifecycle. In Xcode, select File → New → File… and select Source under iOS on the left-hand side. Select the Cocoa Touch Class template and click Next. For the next screen, name the class SessionDelegate and make it a subclass of NSObject. Keep the language as Swift, and then click Next. Make sure that on the next screen the TapALap target is selected, *not* the WatchKit App or WatchKit Extension target. Click Create, and you have your new class. All you need to do is import WatchConnectivity and add conformance to WCSessionDelegate in its declaration:

Chapter 8/TapALap/TapALap/SessionDelegate.swift

```
import WatchConnectivity

class SessionDelegate: NSObject, WCSessionDelegate {
```

 Joe asks:
Why Did We Choose NSObject?

Even though we're writing this app in Swift, we'll occasionally need to pay our respects to Objective-C, the language that predated it for iOS and OS X development. Since the WCSessionDelegate protocol that we're going to conform to was written in Objective-C, it specified that the protocol also conforms to the NSObject protocol. Here's the declaration in Objective-C:

```
@protocol WCSessionDelegate <NSObject>
```

In Swift, this gets translated as such:

```
public protocol WCSessionDelegate : NSObjectProtocol
```

If we wanted to keep our objects as "pure" Swift objects, we could simply conform to NSObjectProtocol ourselves, but then we'd have to implement a whole host of boilerplate methods that we don't really need. By subclassing NSObject instead, we get those methods for free and can focus on the ones that matter for this app.

You'll add more functionality to the session delegate as you go, but before it can do anything, you need to tell the iOS app to start it at launch. Open AppDelegate.swift and add some setup code to application(_:didFinishLaunchingWithOptions:) to kick off your session delegate:

```
import WatchConnectivity

@UIApplicationMain
class AppDelegate: UIResponder, UIApplicationDelegate {

    var window: UIWindow?

    lazy var sessionDelegate = SessionDelegate()

    func application(application: UIApplication,
        didFinishLaunchingWithOptions launchOptions: [NSObject: AnyObject]?)
        -> Bool {
            if WCSession.isSupported() {
                let session = WCSession.defaultSession()

                session.delegate = sessionDelegate
                session.activateSession()
            }

            return true
    }

}
```

When the app starts up, you'll see if WCSession is supported—this will return false on devices that can't pair with Apple Watch, like iPads and iPod Touches. If it's supported, you'll call activateSession() on the session after setting up a delegate for it. This opens up a channel of communication between the watch and the phone, which you'll use as you send data back and forth. First, you'll send the list of tracks back and forth using the *application context*.

Synchronizing Data with the Application Context

Think of the application context like NSUserDefaults; it's a Dictionary that you can treat as an arbitrary key-value store. The application context is a great way to provide data to the counterpart app without interrupting what the user is doing—the data is sent in the background. To update the application context, simply call updateApplicationContext(_:) on your WCSession, passing in the new context in its entirety. The counterpart app can access it with the session's receivedApplicationContext property, as well as through the WCSessionDelegate method session(_:didReceiveApplicationContext:). You will use the application context for the list of tracks.

Sending Tracks to iOS from watchOS

The first step in this app will be to send the tracks to iOS from watchOS whenever they're updated. Open Track.swift to make the necessary modifications. First, you need to import WatchConnectivity:

Chapter 8/TapALap/TapALap WatchKit Extension/Track.swift

```
import WatchConnectivity
```

Next, you modify save() to update the application context:

Chapter 8/TapALap/TapALap WatchKit Extension/Track.swift

```
func save() {
    var tracks = Track.savedTracks()

    guard !tracks.contains(self) else { return }

    tracks.append(self)

    let trackDictionaries: [[String: AnyObject]] = tracks.map {
        $0.dictionaryRepresentation()
    }

    do {
        let newContext = ["Tracks": trackDictionaries]

        try WCSession.defaultSession().updateApplicationContext(newContext)
    }
    catch let error {
        NSLog("Error saving tracks to application context: \(error).")
    }

    NSUserDefaults.standardUserDefaults().setObject(trackDictionaries,
        forKey: "SavedTracks")
}
```

Build and run, and then save a new track. You'll see an error appear in the application's console in Xcode that looks something like this:

```
TapALap WatchKit Extension Error saving tracks to application context:
Error Domain=WCErrorDomain Code=7004 "WatchConnectivity session has not
been activated." UserInfo={NSLocalizedRecoverySuggestion=Activate the
WatchConnectivity session., NSLocalizedDescription=WatchConnectivity session
has not been activated., NSLocalizedFailureReason=Function activateSession
has not been called.}.
```

The important thing to take from this error is "Function activateSession has not been called." Just as you need to start the session on iOS, you need to start it on watchOS, too. You'll use your ExtensionDelegate to create the session. Open up ExtensionDelegate.swift and import WatchConnectivity. Then, add another method to applicationDidFinishLaunching() to start the session:

```
func applicationDidFinishLaunching() {
    startSession()
    returnToInProgressRun()
}

lazy var sessionDelegate = SessionDelegate()

func startSession() {
    WCSession.defaultSession().delegate = sessionDelegate
    WCSession.defaultSession().activateSession()
}
```

You may notice that this code fails to compile. The session needs a delegate to be set before you can call activateSession() on it, and so you've included your SessionDelegate class. Problem is, since you added that class to the iOS App target and not the WatchKit Extension target, it's not available from the latter. To fix that, open SessionDelegate.swift and open Xcode's Utilities pane to the File Inspector (or press ⌘⌥1). Under Target Membership, ensure both targets are checked, like so:

Now, your SessionDelegate class will build for both iOS and watchOS. Build and run again and save a track, and you won't see any errors in the console. Now let's head over to the iOS app and read this data in.

Displaying Tracks on iOS

Your iOS app will begin as simply as it can: a single table view. The Xcode template we used to create TapALap included a view controller, but you're not going to use it. Go ahead and delete ViewController.swift, and then open Main.storyboard (be sure to open the iOS storyboard and not the watchOS storyboard named Interface.storyboard). Delete the existing view controller, and you have a fresh slate to start with. Add a table view controller to the storyboard; this will be your main user interface. Select the table view controller; then open the Attributes Inspector (⌘⌥4) and check the box next to Is Initial View Controller. Next, select the table view itself. There's a prototype cell in there that you don't need; set Prototype Cells to 0 to remove it. Finally, select the view controller, and in Xcode select Editor → Embed In → Navigation Controller. This will add a navigation controller to your UI, which will prevent the table view from appearing behind the status bar. Double-click the title area of the navigation bar to give the view controller the title Tracks. With that, your UI is complete! It should look like the following image:

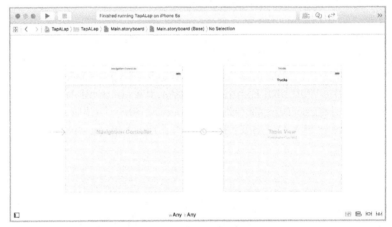

Now you need to get data out of the application context. Create a new Cocoa Touch class for the iOS app, make it a subclass of UITableViewController, and name it TrackListTableViewController. Be sure to open the storyboard and set the class of your new view controller to this new class! Then, in TrackListTableViewController.swift, let's get your list of tracks going! First, you need to import WatchConnectivity:

Chapter 8/TapALap/TapALap/TrackListTableViewController.swift

```swift
import WatchConnectivity
```

Next, you need a way to get tracks out of the application context's data:

Chapter 8/TapALap/TapALap/TrackListTableViewController.swift

```swift
var tracks: [Track] {
    guard let trackDictionaries = WCSession.defaultSession()
        .receivedApplicationContext["Tracks"] as? [[String: AnyObject]]
        else { return [] }

    return trackDictionaries.flatMap(Track.init).sort { $0.name < $1.name }
```

This code will get the Dictionary representations of tracks you saved to the application context and convert them to Track objects. To use them, implement the UITableView data source protocol:

Chapter 8/TapALap/TapALap/TrackListTableViewController.swift

```swift
override func tableView(tableView: UITableView,
    numberOfRowsInSection section: Int) -> Int {
        return tracks.count
}

override func tableView(tableView: UITableView,
    cellForRowAtIndexPath indexPath: NSIndexPath) -> UITableViewCell {
        let reuseIdentifier = "TrackCell"

        let cell: UITableViewCell

        if let reusedCell = tableView.dequeueReusableCellWithIdentifier(
            reuseIdentifier) {
                cell = reusedCell
        }
        else {
            cell = UITableViewCell(style: .Value1,
                reuseIdentifier: reuseIdentifier)
        }

        if tracks.count > indexPath.row {
            let track = tracks[indexPath.row]

            cell.textLabel?.text = track.name

            cell.detailTextLabel?.text = NSLengthFormatter()
                .stringFromMeters(track.lapDistance)
        }

        return cell
}
```

First, you'll return the number of tracks when asked how many rows there are. Next, you'll return a cell for each Track, using the name and the lap distance in the cell. You used a built-in table view cell style, so you don't even need to add any UI! Before you can build this, however, there's a problem—you don't have access to the Track class! As with SessionDelegate.swift, you'll need to open Track.swift and add it to both the WatchKit Extension target and the iOS App target.

Handling Common Code Between Targets

So far, you've been sharing code between targets by including the source files in each. While this works in this case, since there are only two such files, it doesn't really scale to large projects with hundreds of files. In real code, you could use a *framework* target to share this code, keep it organized, and build it for multiple platforms. For more information on creating your own frameworks, consult the Xcode documentation.

At this point, if you build and run the app, you'll see your tracks listed, as you can see here!

Responding to Context Changes

When the application context changes while the iPhone app's session is active, you should update this table view. The easiest way to do that is to use NSNotificationCenter to post a notification whenever it changes. You'll listen for these notifications in viewDidLoad() so that whenever a change occurs, your table view is updated:

Chapter 8/TapALap/TapALap/TrackListTableViewController.swift

```swift
override func viewDidLoad() {
    super.viewDidLoad()
}

func registerForTrackNotifications() {
    NSNotificationCenter.defaultCenter().addObserver(self,
        selector: "applicationContextChanged",
        name: "ApplicationContextChanged",
        object: nil)
}

func applicationContextChanged() {
    NSOperationQueue.mainQueue().addOperationWithBlock {
        self.tableView.reloadData()
    }
}
```

In this code, you simply register for a notification and then call reloadData() on your table view when one comes in. You use NSOperationQueue to make sure that the update happens on the main queue, which is required for UI updates like this. WatchConnectivity doesn't guarantee that the context will be received on the main queue, so this is an important step.

Next, you need to implement the session delegate's side of things. Open SessionDelegate.swift and implement session(_:didReceiveApplicationContext:) to post the notification:

Chapter 8/TapALap/TapALap/SessionDelegate.swift

```
func session(session: WCSession,
    didReceiveApplicationContext applicationContext: [String : AnyObject]) {
        NSNotificationCenter.defaultCenter().postNotificationName(
            "ApplicationContextChanged", object: nil)
}
```

Build and run again. While the iOS app is open, open the watch app and add a track. You'll see the table view update with the new track. Huzzah!

As you can see, the application context is a great way to synchronize data between the iPhone and Apple Watch. Everything you've done so far applies equally in reverse; the iPhone can send a context to the watch for processing in just the same way. Next, let's look at another way to send data back and forth: *user info transfers.*

Transferring One-Way Data with User Info Transfers

If the application context is meant as a shared key-value store to use between the apps, the concept of transferring *user info* between them is the opposite. This API allows you to send a Dictionary of data from one device to other completely asynchronously. Simply use WCSession's transferUserInfo(_:) method, passing in a Dictionary with whatever data you want to send. These user info dictionaries are queued on the sending device, so even if the user quits the watch app before it finishes, watchOS will ensure that the transfer happens when possible. You can inspect the session's outstandingUserInfoTransfers property to see if the transfer has finished, but typically you won't need to—just set it and forget it. On the receiving end, the session's delegate will receive the session(_:didReceiveUserInfo:) method on a background thread with the user info dictionary you passed in. This is especially helpful when the watch and phone aren't connected but then become connected later—whatever data was queued for transmission is sent and handled at the system's convenience. You'll use that in TapALap to handle deleting tracks on the phone.

Deleting Tracks on the iPhone

To handle deleting tracks, you'll use the standard iOS swipe-to-delete and Edit button approach to deleting table view cells. First, let's enable the Edit button. Open up TrackListTableViewController.swift and add it to viewDidLoad():

Chapter 8/TapALap/TapALap/TrackListTableViewController.swift

```
override func viewDidLoad() {
    super.viewDidLoad()
    registerForTrackNotifications()

    navigationItem.rightBarButtonItem = self.editButtonItem()
}
```

This will add the Edit button to the top right of the view controller. When the user taps it, the table view cells will reveal a Delete button. Next, to enable swipe-to-delete, you'll implement tableView(_:canEditRowAtIndexPath:) to tell the system that the rows are editable.

Chapter 8/TapALap/TapALap/TrackListTableViewController.swift

```
override func tableView(tableView: UITableView,
    canEditRowAtIndexPath indexPath: NSIndexPath) -> Bool {
        return true
}
```

Finally, you need to actually delete the tracks when the user tries to delete them. You'll use transferUserInfo(_:) to achieve this—when the user deletes a track, you'll send the track's dictionary representation associated with the key TrackToDelete. You'll add this to tableView(_:commitEditingStyle:forRowAtIndexPath:) and it'll be called when the user taps Delete:

Chapter 8/TapALap/TapALap/TrackListTableViewController.swift

```
override func tableView(tableView: UITableView,
    commitEditingStyle editingStyle: UITableViewCellEditingStyle,
    forRowAtIndexPath indexPath: NSIndexPath) {
        if editingStyle == .Delete {
            let track = tracks[indexPath.row]

            WCSession.defaultSession().transferUserInfo(
                ["TrackToDelete": track.dictionaryRepresentation()])

            tableView.deleteRowsAtIndexPaths([indexPath],
                withRowAnimation: .Automatic)
        }
}
```

If you build and run and then try to delete a track, you'll see a crash. Why? When this method finishes, it tells the table view to delete that row. The problem is, when you delete a row, UITableView expects to get a different result from calling tableView(_:numberOfRowsInSection:) on its data source. Your application context hasn't yet changed—you just sent the info to the watch—so your number of tracks will still include the just-being-deleted one. What can you do to solve this? Simple: you will remove any of the tracks that are pending deletion from the list of tracks. Modify the tracks computed property like so to achieve this:

Chapter 8/TapALap/TapALap/TrackListTableViewController.swift

```
Line 1  var tracks: [Track] {
            guard let trackDictionaries = WCSession.defaultSession()
                .receivedApplicationContext["Tracks"] as? [[String: AnyObject]]
                else { return [] }
5
            let pendingDeletedTracks = WCSession.defaultSession()
                .outstandingUserInfoTransfers
                .map { $0.userInfo }
                .flatMap { $0["TrackToDelete"] as? [String: AnyObject] }
10              .flatMap(Track.init)

            return trackDictionaries.flatMap(Track.init).sort { $0.name < $1.name }
                .filter { !pendingDeletedTracks.contains($0) }
        }
```

This new logic is a little complicated, so let's step through it line-by-line. On line 7, you get an array from the current WCSession of all outstanding user info transfers. Then, on line 8, you transform that array into an array of those transfers' userInfo dictionaries. You know that you used the TrackToDelete key in your user info dictionary, so on line 9 you transform the array again, pulling out whatever was saved under that key as long as it's the correct type. In this case, it'll be the track's dictionary representation. Finally, on line 10, you transform the array one last time into an array of Track objects. With this array, on line 13, you can filter out tracks that are pending deletion. Build and run again, and you can successfully delete tracks! If you launch the app a second time, you'll see any tracks you deleted reappear. Let's switch back over to the watch side so you can actually delete these tracks.

Receiving User Info Transfers on the Watch

Back in your watch app, you will receive these user info transfers in your session delegate. Specifically, the method to implement is session(_:didReceiveUserInfo:). You only want to implement this on watchOS, but since your SessionDelegate class spans both OSes, you can use a conditional to compile it only for watchOS:

Chapter 8/TapALap/TapALap/SessionDelegate.swift

```
#if os(watchOS)
func session(session: WCSession,
    didReceiveUserInfo userInfo: [String : AnyObject]) {
        if let trackDict = userInfo["TrackToDelete"] as? [String: AnyObject],
            track = Track(dictionaryRepresentation: trackDict) {
                track.delete()
        }
}
#endif
```

In this method, if you find a track to delete, you convert the dictionary representation to a Track instance and then call delete() on it. As of now, that doesn't exist, so let's head over to Track.swift and implement it. You can reuse a lot of logic from the existing save() method, so you'll extract some logic out of it. While you're at it, since you can modify the saved tracks only on watchOS, you'll restrict it to watchOS. So, you'll implement save() and delete() as follows:

Chapter 8/TapALap/TapALap WatchKit Extension/Track.swift

```
#if os(watchOS)

func save() {
    var tracks = Track.savedTracks()

    guard !tracks.contains(self) else { return }

    tracks.append(self)

    Track.saveTracks(tracks)
}

func delete() {
    var tracks = Track.savedTracks()

    guard let trackIndex = tracks.indexOf(self) else { return }

    tracks.removeAtIndex(trackIndex)

    Track.saveTracks(tracks)
}

static func saveTracks(tracks: [Track]) {
    let trackDictionaries: [[String: AnyObject]] = tracks.map {
        $0.dictionaryRepresentation()
    }

    do {
        let newContext = ["Tracks": trackDictionaries]

        try WCSession.defaultSession().updateApplicationContext(newContext)
    }
    catch let error {
        NSLog("Error saving tracks to application context: \(error).")
    }
```

```
    NSUserDefaults.standardUserDefaults().setObject(trackDictionaries,
        forKey: "SavedTracks")
}
#endif
```

Each of those methods simply modifies the saved tracks and calls the new saveTracks(_:) method you created. Now, if you run the watch app, then start the iPhone app and delete tracks, you'll be able to delete tracks and have your changes persist. Wonderful!

User info transfers are an excellent choice for sending data back and forth between your apps. You can send as many as you need, and unlike the application context, a new user info dictionary doesn't overwrite the previous one—you simply receive both. This makes it perfect to record that an event happened. Because these transfers are performed in the background, the system can choose when to send them, optimizing battery life on the watch without you even needing to write any code. Sometimes, however, you want to send a message to the counterpart app immediately and even get a response. For that, WatchConnectivity has another trick up its sleeve: sending messages.

Sending Messages in WatchConnectivity

In the early days of WatchKit, before the WatchKit extension ran on the watch itself, all processing happened on the phone. The APIs available to WatchKit extensions were limited, and networking was discouraged. Instead, developers were encouraged to send messages to the parent iOS application, which would process the messages (in the background if necessary) and send a reply. Although those methods are now deprecated in watchOS 2, there are still times when the process is necessary. Sending messages to the phone is a bit like communicating with a web server over HTTP; watchOS and iOS communicate via Dictionary objects sent back and forth. One side—either the watch or the phone—sends a dictionary to the other side, which sends back a reply containing another dictionary. It's a simple process, but it allows you to very easily hand responsibility for a task from the watch to the phone.

When do you use these methods? If a watch app needs more processing power, it's better to perform the computation on the user's iPhone, which has a relatively beefy processor and battery when compared to the minuscule watch components. Even some tasks that are trivial computationally rely on frameworks that are unavailable on the watch and therefore must be performed on the phone. watchOS does some of this itself; since there's no GPS on the watch, it uses the phone's GPS location for the Maps app.

To send a message to the counterpart app, either from iOS or from watchOS, you call WCSession's sendMessage(_:replyHandler:errorHandler:) method. The message parameter is a simple Dictionary containing whatever keys and values you want to send. The counterpart app's session delegate receives the message in the callback method session(_:didReceiveMessage:replyHandler:). When the counterpart is finished with the message, it calls the replyHandler, a closure you provide in the first step. This closure *also* takes a dictionary, which can contain a reply message. If something goes wrong sending the message, your errorHandler will be called.

So, for example, let's say you wanted to make a calculator on watchOS but do all of the actual calculations on iOS, since the phone's processor is so much faster. On the watch, you'd send a message to the phone to add two numbers:

```
func sendMessageToPhone() {
    WCSession.defaultSession().sendMessage(["Add": [2, 2]],
        replyHandler: { (response: [String : AnyObject]) -> Void in
            NSLog("The result is \(response["result"])")
        }, errorHandler: { (error: NSError) -> Void in
            NSLog("An error occurred sending the message: \(error)")
    })
}
```

Then, on the phone, you'd receive this message and reply:

```
func session(session: WCSession,
    didReceiveMessage message: [String : AnyObject],
    replyHandler: ([String : AnyObject]) -> Void) {
        if let numbersToAdd = message["Add"] as? [Int] {
            let sumOfNumbers = numbersToAdd.reduce(0, combine: +)

            replyHandler(["result": sumOfNumbers])
        }
        else {
            replyHandler([:])
        }
}
```

This code adds the numbers using reduce(_:combine:) and then executes the replyHandler with the result. It's important to note that it calls the replyHandler no matter what—if you don't execute it, then the system doesn't know when you've finished.

When you send a message from watchOS to iOS, the parent iOS application wakes up in the background to handle the message. But because the Apple Watch is so constrained on battery life and processing power, sending a message from iOS to watchOS will succeed only if the watch app is open. For that reason, it's much more common to send messages from watchOS to iOS. Next, let's look at a way to send even more data at once.

Sending Files Back and Forth

As if you didn't already have enough ways to transfer data back and forth, there's one more in WatchConnectivity: you can transfer entire files. This may seem like overkill on the watch, which doesn't really have the screen space for editing documents and the like, but it does have one great use case: media. Whether you're recording audio on the watch and transferring it to the phone or transferring (hopefully short) videos from the phone to the watch, these methods allow you to perform those transfers one file at a time using a pretty simple API. From the *sending* device, call transferFile(_:metadata:) on the WCSession. This will add a new WCSessionFileTransfer instance to the outstandingFileTransfers of the session and initiate the transfer when appropriate. On the receiving device, assuming everything went well, the session delegate receives the session(_:didReceiveFile:) method, passing in the path to the file. Be sure to move the file out from this path, because once this method returns, the OS will delete it! Back on the sending app, either after a successful transfer or an error, the session delegate receives the session(_:didFinishFileTransfer:error:) callback method. Use this method to retry if needed. While these file-transferring methods may not be used the most often in your app, they're the most convenient way to send large chunks of data back and forth between devices.

Wrap-Up

Apple Watch and iPhone are two tightly integrated products, and it really shows in the WatchConnectivity framework. In this chapter, you learned how Apple Watch communicates with the world around it, either through Watch-Connectivity or through the network in general. For WatchConnectivity, you saw a number of ways to move data back and forth: sending messages, using the application context, transferring user info, and sending files. With this smorgasbord of methods for moving bits, there's sure to be something that fits the need of your app. Next, let's use this knowledge to power one of the coolest features introduced with watchOS 2: your own watch complications.

Creating Complications with ClockKit

You've learned a lot so far about making apps for the Apple Watch. These apps are great, but given that the Apple Watch is, well, a *watch*, aren't there some watch-specific things we can do in our apps? The answer is an absolute yes. Many of the watch faces available on Apple Watch support *complications*, which are small pieces of data that appear on the watch face. The term *complication* is borrowed from the traditional watchmaking world. A diver's watch, for instance, might feature a depth meter in addition to displaying the time. This depth meter is a complication. On Apple Watch, complications are extremely powerful, delivering bite-sized pieces of information to our users whenever they so much as check the time. In this chapter, you'll learn about the *ClockKit* framework, which you can use to create complications for your own apps!

Apple Watch has a handful of built-in watch faces for users to choose from, and only some of those support third-party complications: Utility, Modular, Simple, Color, and Chronograph (shown in the figure on page 114). For those watch faces, the user can choose individual complications to use at various positions, and that's where you come in. By providing your own complication using ClockKit, your app will appear in the list of complications, allowing users to install your app right on their watch face. This is prime real estate for any app, since these complications appear every time users raise their wrist to look at the watch.

In this chapter, we'll cover creating complications, providing data to them, and providing different complications for different watch faces.

Watch Faces and Complications

One of the first questions to ask when supporting ClockKit complications is simple: *What data should I show?* In the case of TapALap, you could show

Figure 3—The Apple Watch faces that support third-party complications, from left to right: Utility, Modular, Simple, Color, and Chronograph

your most recent run, how fast you ran, and how far, but that's only relevant for the time period during and immediately after the run itself. A great complication has relevant data to show the user at all times. Since any runner needs to stay hydrated and eat regular meals, you can offer a counterpart app focused on those aspects of training. In this chapter we'll develop an app called NomNomNom that shows the user two points of data: how much water he's consumed today and when his next meal is. You could build these features into TapALap itself, but you'd run the risk of cluttering it with too many features—better to keep TapALap focused on running.

The constant availability of complications comes with development challenges: your complication's data needs to be up to date at all times, ready whenever the user needs it, but keeping your WatchKit extension active in the background to constantly update that data would drain the watch's battery quicker than mining Dogecoin.

When it comes to creating these complications, there are five *families* of complication to choose from, depending on the user's chosen watch face. For each of these families, your app selects a *template* and can provide images, text, or both to finish the complication UI. Instead of drawing directly to the screen, these templates take information you pass in, the size of the complication, and the color the user has selected for his watch face to draw itself. This allows the complication to look the part on the watch face without you having to write theme code yourself.

Modular Small complication family (Modular watch face)						
Columns Text	Ring Image	Ring Text	Simple Image	Simple Text	Stack Image	Stack Text

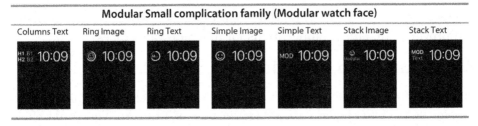

Modular Large complication family (Modular watch face)

| Columns | Standard Body | Table | Tall Body |

Utilitarian Small complication family (Chronograph watch face)

| Ring Image | Ring Text | Simple Image | Small Flat |

Utilitarian Small complication family (Utility watch face)

| Ring Image | Ring Text | Simple Image | Small Flat |

Utilitarian Small complication family (Simple watch face)

| Ring Image | Ring Text | Simple Image | Small Flat |

Utilitarian Large complication family (Utility watch face)

Large Flat

Circular Small complication family (Color watch face)

| Ring Image | Ring Text | Simple Image | Simple Text | Stack Image | Stack Text |

That's a lot of options! Which should you support? In short: as many as you can. You don't know which watch face your users will be using, and you certainly can't ask them to switch just to support your app, so even though the Modular Large family is appealing—if for its sheer size than for no other reason—you'll want to give the user as much choice as possible. It'll be too hard for you to support the smaller complication families, but you can support both large families, which allows your app to run on multiple watch faces.

Providing Complications in Your App

Make a new project for this app using the iOS App with WatchKit App template. In the New Project dialog, be sure to check the box next to Include Complication, because this will create the infrastructure you need to begin providing complication data. This project is going to focus on reading food-related events from the user's calendar, so name it "NomNomNom."

When your project is created by Xcode, it has an empty iPhone app, a WatchKit app, and a WatchKit extension, just as you'd expect. Inside the WatchKit extension are three classes: an empty interface controller named InterfaceController, an empty extension delegate named ExtensionDelegate, and a class named ComplicationController that conforms to the CLKComplicationDataSource protocol. As the name suggests, this protocol is the communication channel through which you'll give the system your complication data. This class, unlike the others in the Xcode template, is preloaded with all of the methods you'll need to implement to get your complications working.

As you start to look at the methods in the CLKComplicationDataSource protocol, you'll notice that they all have one thing in common: their final parameter is named handler and is a closure that takes some form of data. You'll be using these handlers to send data back to the system. When the user selects your app for his complication, watchOS will create an instance of your Complication-Controller class and call these methods to get the complication data. This API design, where the system is responsible for initiating the retrieval of complication data, helps to limit power consumption and streamline the complication-loading process. But how does watchOS know which class to instantiate? To explain that, let's look at more work the template has done on your behalf.

Select the NomNomNom project from Xcode's Project Navigator (⌘1); then select the NomNomNom WatchKit Extension target from the list of targets. Under the General tab, the Complications Configuration section is where the metadata for your complications is stored. The Data Source Class setting is what tells watchOS which class it should instantiate to get complication data.

Any class that conforms to CLKComplicationDataSource will do here; the Complication-Controller class that Xcode created is just a convenience.

Next on this screen is a list of Supported Families. These check boxes indicate which complication families your app supports; since you want your users to be able to select your app's complication from any watch face, leave them all checked. With this data in place, you're ready to start your app.

Providing Your First Complication

Your complication shows users their food schedule. You'll filter their calendar for events with words like *breakfast*, *brunch*, *lunch*, *supper*, and *dinner* in the title. To get access to the user's calendar, you'll use the *EventKit* framework. On watchOS, access to the user's calendar is read-only, but that's fine for your needs. To find the next meal event for the current day, you'll add a new extension to the EKEventStore in EventKit that returns the next food-related event in the current day.

To find out what "the current day" is, you'll need to do some date math. Specifically, you'll need to find out when the next and previous midnight are for a given date, so that you can filter events between those dates. Create a new Swift file in this project called DateMath.swift and create an NSDate extension with these two methods in it:

Chapter 9/NomNomNom/NomNomNom WatchKit Extension/DateMath.swift

```
Line 1  import Foundation

        extension NSDate {
            var midnightBefore: NSDate {
     5          let calendar = NSCalendar.currentCalendar()

                let components = calendar.components([.Year, .Month, .Day, .Hour, .Minute,
                    .Second], fromDate: self)

    10          components.hour   = 0
                components.minute = 0
                components.second = 0

                return calendar.dateFromComponents(components)!
    15      }

            var midnightAfter: NSDate {
                let calendar = NSCalendar.currentCalendar()

    20          let components = calendar.components([.Year, .Month, .Day, .Hour, .Minute,
                    .Second], fromDate: self)

                components.hour   = 0
```

```
25        components.minute = 0
          components.second = 0

          let midnightOf = calendar.dateFromComponents(components)!

          let oneDayComponents = NSDateComponents()
30        oneDayComponents.day = 1

          return calendar.dateByAddingComponents(oneDayComponents, toDate: midnightOf,
              options: NSCalendarOptions())!
      }
35  }
```

If this code looks a little heavy handed for something that seems simple, don't worry—that's emblematic of date- and time-handling code in general. First, on line 7 you extract components of the date from the current calendar. This does assume that you're working in the user's time zone, but since this is for a watch that's likely already set to the correct time zone, it'll work for you. Once you have these components, lines 10, 11, and 12 take the hour, minute, and second values and reset them to 0. This gives you midnight at the beginning of the day, and on line 14 you use those components to create a new NSDate representing it. To get midnight at the *end* of the day, you need to add a day to midnightOf, so you create a new NSDateComponents instance on line 29 and set its day property to 1. Finally, on line 32, you return a new date created by adding oneDayComponents to midnightOf.

Now that you can use your date code, you can write a method on EKEventStore to find food-like events in the user's calendar. You'll add an extension to ComplicationController.swift:

Chapter 9/NomNomNom/NomNomNom WatchKit Extension/ComplicationController.swift

```
Line 1  import EventKit

        extension EKEventStore {
            func requestNextMealEvent(forDate date: NSDate = NSDate(),
5               handler: EKEvent? -> Void) {
                    requestAccessToEntityType(.Event) { (success, error) in
                        if success {
                            let timePredicate = self.predicateForEventsWithStartDate(date,
                                endDate: date.midnightAfter, calendars: nil)
10
                            let mealPredicates = ["breakfast", "brunch", "lunch", "supper",
                                "dinner", "snack", "coffee", "tea", "happy hour", "drinks"]
                                .map { NSPredicate(format: "title contains[cd] %@", $0) }

15                          let mealMatchingPredicate = NSCompoundPredicate(
                                orPredicateWithSubpredicates: mealPredicates)
```

```
            let events = self.eventsMatchingPredicate(timePredicate)
                .filter { mealMatchingPredicate.evaluateWithObject($0) }
                .sort { return $0.startDate.compare($1.startDate) ==
                    .OrderedAscending }

            handler(events.first)
        }
        else {
            handler(nil)
        }
    }
}
}
```

This method takes an NSDate parameter, defaulting to the current date, and a closure to handle success or failure. You can't just return a calendar event—represented by the EKEvent class in EventKit—because the APIs you're using will be asynchronous. The first thing you need to do is request access to the user's events, done on line 6. The user will need to authorize this app before you can access any events, which we'll cover later in this chapter. Next, on line 8, you create a special NSPredicate to filter calendar events between the given date and midnight on that day—which is where your NSDate extension comes in. This predicate will be enough to filter events based on time.

Next, you need to write some more NSPredicates for filtering—this time on the event title. You're looking for food events, so you build an array of food event names on line 11 (feel free to add your own!) and use map() on line 13 to transform them into NSPredicate instances. The [cd] in the predicate text causes the search to be case- and diacritic-insensitive, so "LUNCH" and "Lunch" will both match "lunch." On line 15 you construct one predicate from this array of predicates. By using the NSCompoundPredicate(orPredicateWithSubpredicates:) method, you're making a compound predicate that will match a string including *any* of these terms. This compound predicate is enough to filter events based on title. All that's left is to execute a search.

First, you call eventsMatchingPredicate(predicate:) on line 18 to filter events by date. Next, you use filter() on line 19 to include only those events that match the title search. Then, on line 21, you sort the array by the event's startDate property, making the earliest event the first in the array. When this is done, you can call the callback on line 23 with the first item in the array of events. If nothing matched the search, this may be nil. Finally, in the last else clause on line 26, you call the callback with nil if you couldn't obtain authorization from the user to access their events. This method is now done—given an authorized user, you'll get back the next event that includes food.

With your data in place, you can provide the actual complications to the system. You'll start with the Modular Large complication family. Much like Apple's built-in Calendar complication, yours will display the time of the event and its name. First, you'll implement getCurrentTimelineEntryForComplication(_:handler:) to provide the complication:

```
Line 1  lazy var eventStore = EKEventStore()

        func getCurrentTimelineEntryForComplication(complication: CLKComplication,
            withHandler handler: ((CLKComplicationTimelineEntry?) -> Void)) {
     5
                switch complication.family {
                case .ModularLarge:
                    eventStore.requestNextMealEvent { event in
                        guard let event = event else {
    10                      handler(self.modularLargeTimelineEntryForNoEvents())
                            return
                        }

                        handler(self.modularLargeTimelineEntry(forEvent: event))
    15              }

                default:
                    handler(nil)
                }
    20  }
```

The first thing you do in this function, on line 6, is to switch on the family property of the complication argument you've been passed. Based on the family, which corresponds to the watch face the user has selected and the position of the complication on that face, you'll provide different complications. For now you're going to implement the Modular Large family of complications, but you'll fill in the rest later. For this family, you can display two types of complications: a calendar event regarding food or a message saying there are no more events (much like the built-in Calendar complication). To that end, you request the next event from your event store on line 8. If you don't get an event back, your guard statement on line 9 triggers, and you'll return a timeline entry with a message saying there are no more events. Otherwise, you'll create a timeline entry for the next event and return it. Notice that instead of just using return to return the timeline entry, you invoke handler with it; this allows you to create timeline entries asynchronously, which greatly helps your ability to use frameworks like EventKit. Now that you've written this, you need two methods to return these two timeline entry types. Let's start with modularLargeTimelineEntryForNoEvents():

```
Line 1  func modularLargeTimelineEntryForNoEvents() -> CLKComplicationTimelineEntry {
            let template = CLKComplicationTemplateModularLargeStandardBody()

            template.headerTextProvider = CLKSimpleTextProvider(text:
     5          "Food Calendar")

            template.headerTextProvider.tintColor = .yellowColor()

            template.body1TextProvider = CLKSimpleTextProvider(text:
    10          "No more food today")

            return CLKComplicationTimelineEntry(date: NSDate(),
                complicationTemplate: template)
        }
```

Every complication timeline entry starts with a template in the form of a CLK-ComplicationTemplate subclass. Here you're using CLKComplicationTemplateModularLarge-StandardBody on line 2, which gives you room for header text and one or two lines of body text. To provide this text, instead of simple String properties on the template, you use subclasses of CLKTextProvider. This layer of abstraction allows you to give watchOS more context around the text. For now, you'll just use a CLKSimpleTextProvider to supply a simple string, for both the headerTextProvider and body1TextProvider properties. The CLKComplicationTemplateModularLargeStandardBody template has an optional body2TextProvider property, but if you leave it as nil, the text in body1TextProvider will wrap to both lines of the template. Note also that you supply a tintColor property for the header text provider. In some situations where the user hasn't chosen his watch face's color, you can provide a tint color to use. Feel free to use your brand colors, your app's colors, or whatever looks good—just remember that your users may have settings that result in the tint color you supply being ignored. Finally, on line 12 you create your CLKComplicationTimelineEntry instance, which requires two pieces of data: a date variable, for which you'll simply use the current date, and the complication template itself. The date property is extremely important for the Time Travel feature we'll cover later.

Now that you've finished, you've created a method that returns a template for the case where you can't find any events. Hopefully, you won't need it too often. For the case where you *can* find events on the user's calendar, you'll implement modularLargeTimelineEntry(forEvent:):

```
Line 1  func modularLargeTimelineEntry(forEvent event: EKEvent) ->
            CLKComplicationTimelineEntry {
                let template = CLKComplicationTemplateModularLargeStandardBody()

     5          template.headerTextProvider = CLKTimeIntervalTextProvider(
                    startDate: event.startDate, endDate: event.endDate)

                template.headerTextProvider.tintColor = .yellowColor()

    10          template.body1TextProvider = CLKSimpleTextProvider(text: event.title)

                if let location = event.location {
                    template.body2TextProvider = CLKSimpleTextProvider(text: location)
                }
    15
                return CLKComplicationTimelineEntry(date: event.startDate,
                    complicationTemplate: template)
        }
```

This method begins the same way as modularLargeTimelineEntryForNoEvents(), creating a new CLKComplicationTemplateModularLargeStandardBody, but the text providers you use are very different. Instead of creating a simple, text-only text provider for the header, on line 5 you create a CLKTimeIntervalTextProvider. With this class, you can specify the start and end dates of the EKEvent you're displaying, and the text provider will automatically format the time interval as appropriate for the amount of space you have. In the case of the Modular Large Standard Body complication template, there's plenty of room, so a brunch event from 11:00 a.m. to 1:00 p.m. will appear as "11:00 am - 1:00 pm," all spelled out. As you'll see later in this chapter, other complication templates will format the time differently to fill less space. The other two text providers are just text, so you create them as before. Finally, on line 16, you return a timeline entry for this event. Instead of using NSDate() to get the current date, you use the event's start date as the timeline entry's date. This marks it as beginning when the event began. You could just use the current date here, since you're providing the *current* timeline entry, but it's important to have good data on these entries when it comes to time.

With these methods in place, you're ready to run the app! Build and run the app and you'll be greeted with the black screen shown in the figure. That's OK! Since all of the code you've written so far has been in your ComplicationController, you'll only see it from the watch face. To get there, press ⌘⇧H with your watch simulator open. This simulates pressing the Digital Crown button and thus returns you to the home screen. Click the watch icon to open the watch face. On a real Apple Watch, you configure the watch face by using Force Touch on the watch face, leading to the configuration screens in the following figure. But how do you do a Force Touch on the simulator?

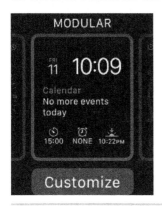  

Figure 4—Configuring the complications of a watch face

To simulate Force Touch, use the Simulator menu option Hardware → Force Touch Pressure → Deep Press (⇧⌘2). This setting acts as a toggle between Shallow Press and Deep Press, so you'll need to do a little back-and-forth dance between them to configure the complication. First, using Deep Press, tap the watch face until the Customize button appears, as in the preceding figure. Switch back to Shallow Press using the menu or ⇧⌘1, and then scroll left and right until you find the Modular watch face. If you don't see it, head to the rightmost screen with the Add button; then tap it and select Modular. When you're on the Modular face and the Customize button is at the bottom, tap it to reveal two pages of configuration. The left page allows you to select the color of the watch face (or Multicolor, which allows the tint color you selected to come through), while the right page allows you to configure the individual complications. Clicking a complication slot moves the selection picker to that slot. For the Modular face, there are four small slots, the time in the upper-right corner (which you can't remove), and one large slot in the middle. The middle one is where your Modular Large template goes, so click that. Scroll up and down with your mouse or trackpad to cycle between the complications. Yours will appear as NomNomNom WatchKit App. Once the watch face is configured to your desire, switch back to a Deep Press to click and exit customization mode, and then switch to Shallow Press to select the watch face (you can also short-circuit this by pressing ⌘⇧H). You're back on the watch and your complication is visible! In all likelihood, you'll see the

"No more food today" message as seen in the following figure, unless your simulator's calendar has some food events on it.

Now that your complication is installed and working, let's make it a little easier to update. In Xcode, click the Scheme List in the toolbar. By default, the WatchKit app scheme is selected, which is why you opened the app to a black screen earlier. Choose the Complication - NomNomNom WatchKit App scheme, then build and run again, and you'll see that the watch simulator opens directly to the complication! It also updates the complication immediately, which is very useful for debugging purposes.

To test the complication, add some data to the simulator's calendar. On the iPhone simulator, open the Calendar app and add a food-related event between now and midnight. Build and run again with the complication scheme selected, and voilà! Your calendar event is now in the complication, as shown in the figure. Now that you've created your complication for the Modular Large family, let's look at providing a complication for another watch face entirely.

Supporting Multiple Complication Families

Luckily, supporting the second complication family isn't going to require anywhere *near* the effort the first one took. You'll be able to reuse a good deal of code. In fact, you'll only need to rewrite the bits that deal with the complication templates themselves. Your second supported family will be for the Utilitarian clock face—the Utilitarian Large template. Like the stock Calendar app, you'll use the text area underneath the Utility watch face's watch face to write a description of the next event. To begin, let's mirror your Modular Large complication methods with a couple of new ones, utilitarianLargeTimelineEntryForNoEvents() and utilitarianLargeTimelineEntry(forEvent:). You'll start with the former:

```
func utilitarianLargeTimelineEntryForNoEvents()
    -> CLKComplicationTimelineEntry {
        let template = CLKComplicationTemplateUtilitarianLargeFlat()

        template.textProvider = CLKSimpleTextProvider(text:
            "No more food today", shortText: "No more food")

        return CLKComplicationTimelineEntry(date: NSDate(),
            complicationTemplate: template)
}
```

Just like the other complication family, this one is fairly straightforward. In fact, it's even easier. Since the Utilitarian Large Flat template has room for only one line of text, you only need to set the textProvider property. This time around, you're creating a CLKSimpleTextProvider with an additional parameter, shortText. This parameter allows watchOS to determine if the string is too long to display, using the shorter variation if necessary. That's it! These three lines are enough for a complication when there are no more events. But what about when there is an event? You have only one line of text to work with, so how will you get all of the relevant data in it?

The answer lies in CLKTextProvider's textProviderWithFormat(_:...) method, which allows you to combine multiple text providers into one! By putting multiple providers together, you can create a text provider that reports both the event time and its title, all on one line. Plus, since the time interval text provider can scale to multiple widths, it will automatically switch its display mode to accommodate longer event titles. Neat! One problem: you can't call this method from Swift. Let's look at how it's declared in Objective-C:

```
+ (CLKTextProvider *)textProviderWithFormat:(NSString *)format, ...
```

It's the ellipsis at the end that gets you. Variadic methods in Objective-C can't be imported directly into Swift, so to use this API, you're going to have to write a little bit of Objective-C. In Xcode, select File → New → File… and choose the Objective-C File template under iOS Source. Set the File Type to Category, the class to CLKTextProvider, and the File to SwiftAdditions. Make sure that the WatchKit Extension target is selected; then click Create. Xcode will ask if you want to make a bridging header to expose Objective-C methods to Swift, as you can see in the screenshot on page 126.

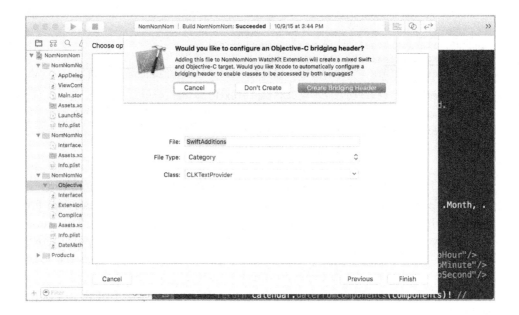

By choosing Create Bridging Header, you will create three new files in the project: CLKTextProvider+SwiftAdditions.h, CLKTextProvider+SwiftAdditions.m, and NomNomNom WatchKit Extension-Bridging Header.h. To be able to use your Objective-C code in Swift, you'll need to add it to the bridging header. Add the following line:

Chapter 9/NomNomNom/NomNomNom WatchKit Extension/NomNomNom WatchKit Extension-Bridging-Header.h

```
#import "CLKTextProvider+SwiftAdditions.h"
```

Now, anything you define in CLKTextProvider+SwiftAdditions.h will be available to your project in Swift. Open that file and declare the method you'll be adding:

Chapter 9/NomNomNom/NomNomNom WatchKit Extension/CLKTextProvider+SwiftAdditions.h

```
NS_ASSUME_NONNULL_BEGIN

@interface CLKTextProvider (SwiftAdditions)

+ (CLKTextProvider *)nnn_textProviderByJoiningProvider:(CLKTextProvider *)provider1
                                          andProvider:(CLKTextProvider *)provider2
                                           withString:(NSString *)string;

@end

NS_ASSUME_NONNULL_END
```

First, you use NS_ASSUME_NONNULL_BEGIN to indicate that the return values and parameters specified below are all assumed to not be nil. This prevents Swift from importing these as implicitly unwrapped optionals or regular optionals, which makes it easier to use. You'll use NS_ASSUME_NONNULL_END at the end to clean this up. Next, you define one method on CLKTextProvider. As is customary in Objective-C, you use a lowercase, three-character prefix on the method name. This prevents problems if future updates or other code creates a method with the same name, since Objective-C doesn't have namespaces. The method, nnn_textProviderByJoiningProvider:andProvider:withString:, will take two CLKTextProvider instances and one NSString. Let's switch over to the implementation file, CLK-TextProvider+SwiftAdditions.m, and implement the method:

Chapter 9/NomNomNom/NomNomNom WatchKit Extension/CLKTextProvider+SwiftAdditions.m

```
@implementation CLKTextProvider (SwiftAdditions)

+ (CLKTextProvider *)nnn_textProviderByJoiningProvider:(CLKTextProvider *)provider1
                                 andProvider:(CLKTextProvider *)provider2
                                 withString:(NSString *)string
{
    return [CLKTextProvider textProviderWithFormat:@"%@%@%@",
            provider1, string, provider2];
}

@end
```

From Objective-C, there's no problem calling textProviderWithFormat: on CLK-TextProvider. The format string you provide has three %@ tokens: one for the first provider, then one for the string that joins the two, and finally one for the second provider. Now that you've added this method, let's go back to the nice, friendly Swift code you've been writing! Return to ComplicationController.swift, where you can finally implement utilitarianLargeTimelineEntry(forEvent:) with your Objective-C helper:

Chapter 9/NomNomNom/NomNomNom WatchKit Extension/ComplicationController.swift

```
func utilitarianLargeTimelineEntry(forEvent event: EKEvent) ->
    CLKComplicationTimelineEntry {
        let template = CLKComplicationTemplateUtilitarianLargeFlat()

        let timeTextProvider = CLKTimeIntervalTextProvider(
            startDate: event.startDate, endDate: event.endDate)
        let titleTextProvider = CLKSimpleTextProvider(text: event.title)

        template.textProvider = CLKTextProvider
            .nnn_textProviderByJoiningProvider(timeTextProvider,
                andProvider: titleTextProvider, withString: " ")

        return CLKComplicationTimelineEntry(date: event.startDate,
            complicationTemplate: template)
}
```

At first, this method seems just like the one you wrote for the Modular watch face. You make a template and then make a pair of text providers for the event's time and title. You combine them into one text provider and then set it as the template's text provider. Now that you have this method implemented, let's get it working. Return to your getCurrentTimelineEntryForComplication(_:handler:) implementation and add another case statement for this family:

```
case .UtilitarianLarge:
    eventStore.requestNextMealEvent { event in
        guard let event = event else {
            handler(self.utilitarianLargeTimelineEntryForNoEvents())
            return
        }

        handler(self.utilitarianLargeTimelineEntry(forEvent: event))
    }
```

Build and run to get back to the watch face. Using a Deep Press touch, customize the watch face, selecting the Utility face and then customizing it to add your complication along the bottom. Huzzah! Your event appears as in the screenshot, with both its time and its title! This is great for text, but what about images? Next, let's look at image support in complications.

Using Images in Complications

So far, your complications have dealt entirely in text. There's nothing wrong with that—they convey plenty of information and look great on the user's watch face. Providing images, however, opens up your app to a wider world of functionality. While the complication families you've seen so far are great for text, the smaller ones on these watch faces are a bit cramped for this kind of information. They can fit a word at best and a few measly characters at worst. When it comes to packing information into a dense space, an image is a great idea.

Just like providing text with a CLKTextProvider, you'll provide images using a CLKImageProvider. These images must be template images—watchOS will use their alpha channel only, drawing them at whatever color the user specifies (for exact image dimensions, refer to the ClockKit documentation). You can provide one-piece or two-piece images; the latter can have a foreground and background image, giving you a two-tone appearance (even though you can't always pick the colors). For some watch faces with a Multicolor option, a tint-Color property is available. Use this to specify the default color for your image, but don't be surprised to see it in another color if the user has one selected. The two-piece images are used only in multicolor environments, so you'll still need to provide a one-piece image.

We've covered providing data for complications, but there are many more methods in CLKComplicationDataSource. Next, let's look at how to control the privacy of complication data.

Managing Complication Privacy

For every complication you provide, it's important to think about its privacy implications. For our water example, it's probably not a big deal if the user's watch is locked but their water consumption is still displayed on the watch face. For a calendar, that can be trickier—you may not want your co-workers to know about your upcoming midnight snack! Other apps are pretty clearly privacy concerns: a complication that shows your bank account balance, for instance, should definitely not display when the user's watch is locked.

One of the CLKComplicationDataSource methods you'll implement in your ComplicationController is getPrivacyBehaviorForComplication(_:withHandler:). The handler for this method takes a CLKComplicationPrivacyBehavior enum, which can be either .ShowOnLockScreen or .HideOnLockScreen. For your app, you'll hide the calendar items, lest someone ends up with a secret meeting visible on their locked device!

Chapter 9/NomNomNom/NomNomNom WatchKit Extension/ComplicationController.swift

```
func getPrivacyBehaviorForComplication(complication: CLKComplication,
    withHandler handler: (CLKComplicationPrivacyBehavior) -> Void) {
        handler(.HideOnLockScreen)
}
```

This method is pretty straightforward, but you're still going to want to test it. Unfortunately, there's no way to display the lock screen on the watch simulator, so to see this in action you'll need to test on a real device. Refer to the section on page 13 on running your app on a hardware watch for more help with that. When disabled, your Modular Large complication looks like the screenshot.

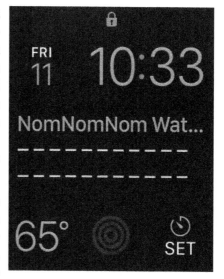

Now that you know how to properly secure your complications, let's look at some other configuration you can do in your app to tailor your complication experience for your users when they go to add your complication to their watch face.

Providing Placeholder Complications

When your users are adding complications to their watch face, they'll see your app by name in the list, sorted alphabetically, as they scroll through the list of supported complications from their apps. On the watch face itself, however, they'll see some placeholder content instead of real content. This is deliberate—notice that while you're configuring the watch face, it sets its time to 10:09, another nod to traditional watchmaking. In the same way, complication placeholder content represents the *typical* content of a complication, not necessarily its *actual* content. It's a chance for you to show your users what the complication is all about, so you should put your best face forward.

The method you'll implement in your ComplicationController class is getPlaceholderTemplateForComplication(_:withHandler:). Instead of being called when the user is actively selecting his complications, the placeholder you create is aggressively cached. watchOS will call this method when your app is *installed* so that by the time the user wants to choose a complication, the placeholder is already up to date. This means, then, that you can't rely on any user data to create the placeholder template, since the app will not have run to ask them for permission. You'll just use the generic calendar template for when there are no food events. Unlike the other methods, you don't return a CLKComplicationTimelineEntry here; since you don't need to provide an NSDate for the timeline entry's time, you simply return a CLKComplicationTemplate:

Chapter 9/NomNomNom/NomNomNom WatchKit Extension/ComplicationController.swift

```swift
func getPlaceholderTemplateForComplication(complication: CLKComplication,
    withHandler handler: (CLKComplicationTemplate?) -> Void) {
        switch complication.family {
        case .ModularLarge:
            handler(modularLargeTimelineEntryForNoEvents().complicationTemplate)
        case .UtilitarianLarge:
            handler(
                utilitarianLargeTimelineEntryForNoEvents().complicationTemplate)
        default:
            handler(nil)
        }
}
```

You can leverage your existing methods and pull out the complicationTemplate property to provide a template. Now that you've done this, you can see your templates in action. Simply choose a different complication, return to the watch face, and then go back to the list of complications. When you scroll to your app, you'll see the template instead of real data! Now your users will be able to see your complication before they commit to using it in one of their scarce complication slots, as the following figure shows. Next up, let's look at how to restrict which watch faces your complication appears on, so that you can avoid someone trying to install it on a watch face you don't support.

Figure 5—Our complication placeholder in the watch face configuration screen

Restricting Complication Families

Sometimes, a particular complication family just doesn't make sense for your data. A complication to show a random inspirational quote probably wouldn't make sense in the Modular Small family. To that end, you can tell watchOS which complication families you support, so that it won't offer your complication to the user on the wrong watch face. In Xcode, open your project settings; then select the NomNomNom WatchKit Extension target. Under the Info tab, there are two key/value pairs of interest. The first, CLKComplicationPrincipalClass, tells watchOS which class it should instantiate to create complication data. In this case, you can leave it at its default value of $(PRODUCT_MODULE_NAME).ComplicationController, which maps to your ComplicationController class.

The second interesting key/value pair is CLKComplicationSupportedFamilies. The value for this key is an array of strings, each representing a supported family. Delete CLKComplicationFamilyModularSmall, CLKComplicationFamilyUtilitarianSmall, and CLKComplicationFamilyCircularSmall to match what you've implemented in the app.

In general, it's good practice to implement as many complication families as you can, but there are certain situations where you may not be able to implement all of them. If that happens, don't sweat it—just edit the project info to hide those families you can't implement.

Wrap-Up

In this chapter, we covered a lot of ground for complications. You created complication templates, both for timeline entries and as placeholders, placed data in those templates, and created timeline entries out of them. You also managed the different complication families on different watch faces, providing the right complication template for each one. Turns out, complications live up to their name! In fact, we haven't covered complications in their entirety yet. In the next chapter, you'll learn about the Time Travel feature in watchOS, which adds another dimension to your complication data by allowing the user to follow it forward and backward in time. You'll also learn how to keep your complication data up to date between app launches and how watchOS rations power use to your apps to prevent you from hogging the entire battery just for your app. See you there!

Extending Complications with Time Travel

When you raise your wrist to look at your Apple Watch, you see the current state of all of your complications, a snapshot of the data you care about *right now*. This is a *smart watch*, though; shouldn't you be able to do more? There is a feature that makes complications—and the apps that support them—even more useful in your daily life. With the watch face activated, turning the Digital Crown activates Time Travel, which lets you see the state of your complications forward or backward in time. This advanced feature of ClockKit is a great use of complications, because it makes more of your users' data available at a moment's notice. In this chapter, we'll look at Time Travel, how to update your complication data once you've provided it, and some of the power restrictions that watchOS has in place to keep your complication from running down the battery. You'll add Time Travel support to your NomNom-Nom sample app to see past and future food-related appointments.

Making Your Complication Excellent with Time Travel

To support Time Travel, you need to modify your ComplicationController in Nom-NomNom to support it. Just as you need to provide the current complication *before* the user raises her wrist, so that the data can be there immediately, you need to provide the past and future complications before the user activates Time Travel, so she can smoothly transition from present to past and future. It all begins with getSupportedTimeTravelDirectionsForComplication(_:withHandler:). This method determines whether your complication can support going forward or backward in time (or both). For NomNomNom, since you're looking at calendar data, you can support both. Other apps may be a judgment call: for instance, should a weather complication support the past so you can see what the temperature was an hour ago? Then there's the obvious joke: figure out how to make a stock market complication support the future, and retire a billionaire. For now, let's implement this method on NomNomNom:

```
func getSupportedTimeTravelDirectionsForComplication(
    complication: CLKComplication,
    withHandler handler: (CLKComplicationTimeTravelDirections) -> Void) {
        handler([.Forward, .Backward])
}
```

Since you support both directions, you pass them both to handler. Now the system will try to display timeline entries for the past and future. Complications that don't support Time Travel in a given direction are grayed out during Time Travel to indicate to the user that they're unavailable.

Next, you need to tell the system the range of dates for which Time Travel is available. If the user advances Time Travel beyond the end date you've specified, your complication will be grayed out to indicate that there's no more data. For you to know the appropriate dates to provide, you're going to need to know when the first and last calendar events are inside the maximum range of Time Travel. Let's build this out, piece by piece.

Finding the Minimum and Maximum Time Travel Dates

You need to find the range of dates that Time Travel supports. No matter what data you provide, the user can only use Time Travel to go from midnight at the beginning of the previous day to midnight at the end of the next day. This gives you a three-day window to work with: yesterday, today, and tomorrow. To represent those dates as NSDate instances, you need to refactor your date math from the last chapter. Open DateMath.swift and modify it as follows:

```
private let calendar = NSCalendar.currentCalendar()

extension NSDate {
    private var componentsAtMidnight: NSDateComponents {
        let components = calendar.components([.Year, .Month, .Day, .Hour, .Minute,
            .Second], fromDate: self)

        components.hour   = 0
        components.minute = 0
        components.second = 0

        return components
    }

    var midnightBefore: NSDate {
        return calendar.dateFromComponents(componentsAtMidnight)!
    }

    func midnightBeforeWithDayOffset(offset: Int) -> NSDate {
        let dayOffsetComponents = NSDateComponents()
```

```
        dayOffsetComponents.day = offset

        return calendar.dateByAddingComponents(dayOffsetComponents,
            toDate: midnightBefore,
            options: NSCalendarOptions())!
    }

    var midnightAfter: NSDate {
        return midnightBeforeWithDayOffset(1)
    }
}
```

In this code, you pull out the bit that creates NSDateComponents for a date at midnight into its own computed property, componentsAtMidnight. The midnightBefore computed property becomes simple: just create a date from those components. midnightAfter is now implemented in terms of midnightBeforeWithDayOffset(_:), which will add (or subtract) days to the midnight components. Using this method, you'll be able to compute the dates for Time Travel.

Back in ComplicationController.swift, let's use this method to find the minimum and maximum dates that Time Travel will cover:

Chapter 10/NomNomNom/NomNomNom WatchKit Extension/ComplicationController.swift

```
var timeTravelBeginDate: NSDate {
    return NSDate().midnightBeforeWithDayOffset(-1)
}
var timeTravelEndDate: NSDate {
    return NSDate().midnightBeforeWithDayOffset(2)
}
```

You use -1 for the beginning offset to subtract one day from midnight of the current day and 2 to add two days to it, giving you the correct dates for Time Travel. Next, let's use those dates to filter your calendar events, so you can find just the calendar events that the user can use Time Travel to get to.

Filtering Calendar Events for Time Travel

Much like your date math, you're going to refactor your EventKit extension to allow you to filter meal events by date. You'll make a new method, get-MealEventsBetweenDate(_:andDate:completion:), which you'll use to filter your events. Refactor the extension as follows:

Chapter 10/NomNomNom/NomNomNom WatchKit Extension/ComplicationController.swift

```
extension EKEventStore {
    func getMealEventsBetweenDate(startDate: NSDate, andDate endDate: NSDate,
        completion: [EKEvent] -> Void) {
            requestAccessToEntityType(.Event) { (success, error) in
                if success {
```

```
                        let timePredicate = self.predicateForEventsWithStartDate(
                            startDate,
                            endDate: endDate,
                            calendars: nil)

                        let mealPredicates = ["breakfast", "brunch", "lunch", "supper",
                            "dinner", "snack", "coffee", "tea", "happy hour", "drinks"]
                            .map { NSPredicate(format: "title contains[cd] %@", $0) }

                        let mealMatchingPredicate = NSCompoundPredicate(
                            orPredicateWithSubpredicates: mealPredicates)

                        let events = self.eventsMatchingPredicate(timePredicate)
                            .filter { mealMatchingPredicate.evaluateWithObject($0) }

                        completion(events)
                    }
                    else {
                        completion([])
                    }
                }
            }
        }

    func requestNextMealEvent(forDate date: NSDate = NSDate(),
        handler: EKEvent? -> Void) {
            getMealEventsBetweenDate(date, andDate: date.midnightAfter) { events in

                let nextEvent = events
                    .sort { $0.startDate.compare($1.startDate) == .OrderedAscending}
                    .first

                handler(nextEvent)
            }
        }
    }
```

All of the logic in getMealEventsBetweenDate(_:andDate:completion:) comes from requestNextMealEvent(forDate:handler:)—events are filtered based on the dates that are passed in and then on the event's title. In requestNextMealEvent(forDate:handler:), you leave the logic for *when* to filter—between now and midnight—as well as the logic to simply return the earliest event, if there is one.

With this method, you can now filter the user's calendar to find all of the events that should show up using Time Travel:

Chapter 10/NomNomNom/NomNomNom WatchKit Extension/ComplicationController.swift

```
func getCalendarEvents(completion: [EKEvent] -> Void) {
    let minimumDate = timeTravelBeginDate
    let maximumDate = timeTravelEndDate

    eventStore.getMealEventsBetweenDate(minimumDate, andDate: maximumDate,
        completion: completion)
}
```

The getCalendarEvents(_:) method computes the beginning and ending dates, filters the events in the calendar to be between them, and then calls completion with the matching events. Even if there are no matching events, you'll still get an array; it'll just be empty. Finally, now that you know the range of events you're supporting, you can implement your complication data source methods to tell ClockKit when Time Travel is supported:

```swift
func getTimelineStartDateForComplication(complication: CLKComplication,
    withHandler handler: (NSDate?) -> Void) {
        getCalendarEvents { events in
            let earliestDate = events.reduce(NSDate()) { (date, event) in
                return date.earlierDate(event.startDate)
            }

            handler(earliestDate)
        }
}

func getTimelineEndDateForComplication(complication: CLKComplication,
    withHandler handler: (NSDate?) -> Void) {
        getCalendarEvents { events in
            let latestDate = events.reduce(NSDate()) { (date, event) in
                return date.laterDate(event.endDate)
            }

            handler(latestDate)
        }
}
```

These methods are similar, just mirror images of one another. The first finds the earliest date of all of the events' start dates, and the second finds the latest date of all of the events' end dates. They use reduce(_:combine:) to iterate through the events' dates, using earlierDate(_:) and laterDate(_:) to find the earlier and later dates of each pair. Now that you have these dates, you can construct new timeline entries for each event!

Returning a Timeline of Events

Time Travel works by moving along a timeline of events, ranging from the beginning date to the end date. As the user moves through events, the *next* event in the timeline is displayed to her. To implement Time Travel, all you need to do is to return CLKComplicationTimelineEntry instances for each event. Let's work on the past first:

```swift
func getTimelineEntriesForComplication(complication: CLKComplication,
    beforeDate date: NSDate,
    limit: Int,
    withHandler handler: (([CLKComplicationTimelineEntry]?) -> Void)) {
        eventStore.getMealEventsBetweenDate(timeTravelBeginDate,
            andDate: date) { events in
                let timelineEntries = events
                    .flatMap { event -> CLKComplicationTimelineEntry? in
                        switch complication.family {
                        case .UtilitarianLarge:
                            return self.utilitarianLargeTimelineEntry(
                                forEvent: event)
                        case .ModularLarge:
                            return self.modularLargeTimelineEntry(
                                forEvent: event)
                        default:
                            return nil
                        }
                    }

                handler(timelineEntries)
        }
}
```

This method is pretty dense, so let's break it down. First, you filter your calendar between the timeline beginning date and the date passed in to this method. This will give you every event before date. When you have those, you use flatMap(_:) to convert the array of EKEvent events into CLKComplicationTimelineEntry classes using the methods you wrote before. Once you have an array of timeline entries, you pass it into the handler, and your Time Travel is ready to go! For future events, you do the same thing:

```swift
func getTimelineEntriesForComplication(complication: CLKComplication,
    afterDate date: NSDate,
    limit: Int,
    withHandler handler: (([CLKComplicationTimelineEntry]?) -> Void)) {
        eventStore.getMealEventsBetweenDate(date,
            andDate: timeTravelEndDate) { events in
                let timelineEntries = events
                    .flatMap { event -> CLKComplicationTimelineEntry? in
                        switch complication.family {
                        case .UtilitarianLarge:
                            return self.utilitarianLargeTimelineEntry(
                                forEvent: event)
                        case .ModularLarge:
                            return self.modularLargeTimelineEntry(
                                forEvent: event)
```

```
                    default:
                        return nil
                    }
                }

                handler(timelineEntries)
        }
}
```

The difference here is simply the order of the dates passed in; this time, you'll go from the given date to the timeline end date. With these two methods in place, you're finished with Time Travel! Build and run, and you can see for yourself. Either manipulate the Digital Crown on a physical device or scroll your trackpad on the simulator to activate Time Travel.

This screenshot shows the same complication in the past, present, and future. As you scroll through time, however, you might notice that the complication behaves slightly differently from the built-in system calendar complication. Whereas the system calendar complication includes an animation while it transitions from event to event, your complication just changes in place; the labels update to reveal their new contents but don't animate at all. You can specify the *animation behavior* of your complication to solve this problem.

Animating Between Complications with Animation Behavior

For your complication, you'd like to have an animated transition between any two timeline entries. To achieve this, you need to implement another callback in your complication controller:

Chapter 10/NomNomNom/NomNomNom WatchKit Extension/ComplicationController.swift

```
func getTimelineAnimationBehaviorForComplication(complication: CLKComplication,
    withHandler handler: (CLKComplicationTimelineAnimationBehavior) -> Void) {
        handler(CLKComplicationTimelineAnimationBehavior.Always)
}
```

By simply calling the handler with .Always, you tell ClockKit to always animate between timeline entries. If you build and run the app, you'll see the behavior as one entry is swapped out for the next during Time Travel. Perfect! If this isn't quite what you want, there are other options available. Passing .Never instead of .Always will remove all animations from the complication. In between these two extremes is .Grouped. This value causes ClockKit to look at the time-lineAnimationGroup property of the CLKComplicationTimelineEntry instances on the timeline. If two entries next to each other in the timeline have different animation groups set, or if one is nil, then the system will use an animation. If the animation groups are the same, then no animation will be performed. This is a great way to get custom behavior out of your timeline.

With these APIs in place, you've completed adding Time Travel support to NomNomNom. Users can see their food calendar for three days at a time right on their watch. Time Travel is real, and you can use it today! Great Scott!

Updating Complications

You've used Time Travel to provide a timeline of complication data, allowing your users to seek forward and backward in time to their hearts' content. What do you do when you need to update this data? Suppose a user adds a new calendar event for a coffee date, or you have a weather app and a new hourly forecast comes out? ClockKit includes multiple methods of updating your complication with new information, so that once you provide an initial set of data, you can add to it or refresh it altogether. Let's go through these methods and see which ones are best for NomNomNom.

Refreshing Data at an Interval

The easiest way to refresh complication data is at an interval. By providing a refresh date to ClockKit, you can get a callback when it's time to provide more data. For NomNomNom, once you provide a timeline of data, unless that data changes, you don't need to update during the day. Compared to a weather app that could update every 15 minutes, your data is relatively unchanging. To that end, you could simply update every night at midnight with a new day's worth of data. To tell ClockKit when to wake up your complication controller to receive new updates, implement getNextRequestedUpdate-DateWithHandler(_:) to provide midnight as the update date:

Chapter 10/NomNomNom/NomNomNom WatchKit Extension/ComplicationController.swift

```
func getNextRequestedUpdateDateWithHandler(handler: (NSDate?) -> Void) {
    handler(NSDate().midnightAfter)
}
```

This code tells ClockKit to request an update at midnight. It's not enough to implement this, however; you need to respond to the update request. When ClockKit wakes up your app to provide additional data, it'll call requestedUpdateDidBegin() on your complication controller. Let's implement that now:

Chapter 10/NomNomNom/NomNomNom WatchKit Extension/ComplicationController.swift

```swift
func requestedUpdateDidBegin() {
    let complicationServer = CLKComplicationServer.sharedInstance()

    for complication in complicationServer.activeComplications {
        complicationServer.extendTimelineForComplication(complication)
    }
}
```

To update your complications, you need to talk to a part of the system you haven't seen yet: the *complication server*. Represented by the CLKComplicationServer class, the complication server is responsible for managing the active complications in the app—that is, the ones the user has installed onto her current watch face. You can query these complications with the activeComplications property, which returns an array of complications for this app that are currently active. Most of the time, there will be only one active complication, but if an app supports multiple complication families on the same watch face, a user could install both simultaneously. For any active complication, you call extendTimelineForComplication(_:) on the complication server, which tells ClockKit to ask for new events beyond the last provided timeline entry. You could also call reloadTimelineForComplication(_:) if you needed to reload the entire timeline; for apps where the data can change once it's created, this is a better option.

Now that you've called extendTimelineForComplication(_:), you're finished! ClockKit will continually update the complication at or around midnight every night, pulling in new calendar entries as needed. NomNomNom doesn't need to update very often, so this is a good solution for you. For other types of apps, let's next look at some other methods of reloading the timeline.

Manually Reloading the Timeline from WatchKit

The CLKComplicationServer class is available from all of WatchKit, not just from your complication controller. From your WatchKit extension, you can query the installed set of complications, as well as call extendTimelineForComplication(_:) or reloadTimelineForComplication(_:) on the complication server. When you call either of those methods from within your WatchKit extension, ClockKit will either extend or reload the timeline. It's possible that this could happen in the background while your watch app is open, so be sure that any common data sources can be read from multiple threads at once!

Why would you want to use manual updates? Any watch app where the complication timeline changes as a result of user activity is a great candidate. For instance, if you implemented a watch app for NomNomNom to add new food-based events to the user's calendar, you could call these methods as new events were added. By proactively reloading your timeline, you can ensure that the data is always relevant when the complication becomes active. Even while the user is using your watch app, the complication can be a mere double-click away, since double-clicking the Digital Crown returns to the watch face and therefore your complications!

Manually Reloading the Timeline from iOS with WatchConnectivity

Reloading the timeline manually from the watch app works for when the user is on her watch, but for when she's on her phone, you can use WatchConnectivity to update your complications. Just as with updating from the WatchKit extension, this is perfect for responding to user interaction by reloading the timeline. There's no CLKComplicationServer to talk to on iOS, so instead use WatchConnectivity's WCSession to send over the new data. Just like transferUserInfo(_:) for sending arbitrary data, WCSession has a complication-specific method, transferCurrentComplicationUserInfo(_:). By calling the latter with complication-specific information, your iOS app can update the complications on its counterpart watchOS app.

When you call transferCurrentComplicationUserInfo(_:), your session delegate handles it the same way as a call to transferUserInfo(_:). You need to implement session(_:didReceiveUserInfo:) and handle the info manually. Once you've handled the information from the iOS app—saved it to your database and the like—you still need to call extendTimelineForComplication(_:) or reloadTimelineForComplication(_:) for any active complication that now has new data, because ClockKit is extremely conservative about calling these methods on your behalf.

If all user info transfers are handled by the same session delegate method, why is there a separate transferCurrentComplicationUserInfo(_:) method on WCSession? As you'll see later in this chapter, ClockKit is aggressive about limiting processing power. Any processing relating to a user info transfer begun with transferCurrentComplicationUserInfo(_:) is "marked" as belonging to the complication controller, and it may impact power use restrictions.

Remotely Reloading the Timeline with Push Notifications

The source of updates for your complications keeps getting farther and farther away from your complication controller. First it was elsewhere in the WatchKit Extension, and then it was in the containing iOS app. You can update the timeline from even farther away: a remote server! This is a great option for apps that rely on a backend service for their data. If you turned NomNomNom into a social calendar for food lovers, you'd want to be able to update your calendar from the website. When that happened, you'd send a push notification to the phone. On the phone, you'd use the PKPushRegistry to register for push notifications of type PKPushTypeComplication. The push registry has a delegate method, pushRegistry(_:didReceiveIncomingPushWithPayload:forType:), that you can implement to handle these notifications. Handling them might look something like this:

```
func pushRegistry(registry: PKPushRegistry!,
    didReceiveIncomingPushWithPayload payload: PKPushPayload!,
    forType type: String!) {
        if type == PKPushTypeComplication {
            let info = ["PushNotificationPayload": payload.dictionaryPayload]

            WCSession.defaultSession().transferCurrentComplicationUserInfo(info)
        }
}
```

Once you receive the notification in your iOS app, you still need to transfer the information to your watchOS app. From there, you can handle the data and update your complications. This is a great option for apps where the data changes frequently or at unpredictable intervals.

With these four methods of updating your complication, you're bound to find something that fits whatever kind of app you're making. ClockKit makes handling updates easy, and the same code that creates your timeline in the first place is automatically used to get future entries. All of this has a cost, however, and ClockKit is always monitoring how much energy your app is using. Next, let's look at how ClockKit handles apps that try to spend too much time updating their information.

Staying Within the Power Budget

If there's a limited resource in ClockKit, it's time. Time spent on the CPU computing complication data causes the watch to lose battery life, and too many complications trying to load too much data would quickly overwhelm the battery and deplete a watch full of third-party complications by midday. To combat this, ClockKit encourages developers to spend as little energy as possible in their complication controllers. It keeps track of how much time each app has spent and gives each of them a *power budget*. Once an app has gone over its daily power budget, it can no longer update its complication until the next day. While that wouldn't be a huge problem for NomNomNom, it could be extremely problematic for other apps—a complication that deals with stock prices, for instance, would be completely useless if it couldn't update after 10 a.m.

To combat the power budget restrictions in ClockKit, you need to do everything in your power to make complication calculations quick. Later you'll find an entire chapter on page 167 about performance in general, but for ClockKit, there are some specific recommendations. First, don't compute anything more than you need to. If you're transferring a userInfo object from iOS, for instance, remove all unnecessary data from the dictionary before sending it across. Instead of making network calls when you update your complication, take advantage of Background App Refresh on iOS to perform expensive network calls when it doesn't affect the complication controller's power budget. Finally, whenever possible, use extendTimelineForComplication(_:) instead of reload-TimelineForComplication(_:); the former will only add new timeline entries, but the latter will re-create existing complications!

There's no way to ask the complication server how much of your power budget you've used up. Once it's up, it's up. You do get one last chance to update your complication, however: when your requested update time is reached, if your budget is exhausted, ClockKit will call requestedUpdateBudgetExhausted() on your complication controller in place of requestedUpdateDidBegin(). This is your last chance to update complications for the day, so the timeline entries you create should not be short-lived. Once this method finishes and your timeline is finalized for the day, you won't receive any more CLKComplicationDataSource() methods until the next day.

Wrap-Up

Complications definitely live up to their name. In the past two chapters, we've gone over creating and customizing complications, allowing the user to scroll through them in time using Time Travel and updating the complications from pretty much anywhere. The inclusion of complications in your app can lead to amazing user engagement—no other system API causes your user to see your app every time she raises her wrist. For that reason, implementing a good complication is one of the best things you can do to make an excellent watch app. Complications are a unique piece of software on watchOS. In the next chapter, we'll look at using some of the hardware on the device: the accelerometer and the heart rate sensor.

Getting Personal with Sensor Data and HealthKit

Now that you've seen the amazing things the Apple Watch can do with touch input, let's go even further. Touching the screen is an important way that users interact with apps, but it's not the only one. In this chapter, we'll look at two more ways that the watch can get data from the user: from its motions through three-dimensional space as recorded by its accelerometer and from the heart rate monitor on the back of the watch. These methods combined can bring an app from a flat, two-dimensional screen to the real world. When you combine the heart rate sensor with HealthKit, an app can become even more: an integral part of your users' lives. As we explore the heart rate sensor, you'll add it to TapALap to bring your running app to the next level. To begin this exploration of the world outside the screen, let's start by using the watch's accelerometer data to manipulate onscreen content.

Getting Device Motion with the CoreMotion Framework

As it does on iOS, the CoreMotion framework allows you to get access to live-updating data of the device's motion through space. As the Apple Watch moves through space, its sensors update data and can call back into your apps. Getting access to this data is as easy as creating a CMMotionManager instance and registering for updates. Unfortunately, as of this writing, the class knows about many more data types than the watch actually supports. The CoreMotion classes on watchOS are analogous to the same classes on iOS, so they have references to data from three sensors: an accelerometer, a gyroscope, and a magnetometer. The data from these three sensors combines into an aggregate data type called simply device motion, which gives a more accurate measurement than the sensors alone. As you can discover yourself by calling accelerometerAvailable(), gyroAvailable(), and related methods, *only* the accelerometer is available on the Apple Watch.

You can take advantage of it for some cool effects. Open up the Soccer project that you made earlier on page 37 and change it to use the accelerometer to move the ball.

Registering for Accelerometer Data Updates

One of the properties of the accelerometer is that it's incredibly noisy, capable of producing data samples at an extremely fast rate. Processing every sample that comes out of it is like trying to drink out of a firehose. Instead of trying to read the raw data off the sensor manually, CoreMotion gives you an interface to *register for updates*. What this means is that you provide CoreMotion with the code to run whenever there's new data (as well as a queue to run the code on), and it will take care of calling that code as new data streams in. Since this code will be called rapidly, you want to make sure it's as fast as possible.

Open InterfaceController.swift in the Soccer WatchKit extension. You'll register for the accelerometer data updates here. Before you can do anything, you'll need to import the CoreMotion framework:

Chapter 11/Soccer/Soccer WatchKit Extension/InterfaceController.swift

```
import CoreMotion
```

The first thing you'll do using CoreMotion is to add a new lazy property for a CMMotionManager that you'll use to do the registration:

Chapter 11/Soccer/Soccer WatchKit Extension/InterfaceController.swift

```
lazy var motionManager = CMMotionManager()
```

With that manager in hand, you'll implement didAppear() and start receiving accelerometer data there. Before you jump in, however, you need a place to store the received data and a queue to process it on. The accelerometer data comes in quickly, so you'll want to process it on a background NSOperationQueue—processing it on the main queue would take up enough processor time that your UI would become unresponsive. Finally, in didDeactivate(), you'll be sure to stop collecting that data. Implement the methods as follows:

Chapter 11/Soccer/Soccer WatchKit Extension/InterfaceController.swift

```
var accelerometerData: CMAcceleration
lazy var motionQueue = NSOperationQueue()

override func didAppear() {
    super.didAppear()

    guard motionManager.accelerometerAvailable else { return }
```

```
    motionManager.startAccelerometerUpdatesToQueue(motionQueue) { data, _ in
        guard let data = data else { return }

        self.accelerometerData = data.acceleration
    }
}

override func didDeactivate() {
    super.didDeactivate()

    if motionManager.accelerometerActive {
        motionManager.stopAccelerometerUpdates()
    }
}
```

The key to this method is the call to startAccelerometerUpdatesToQueue(_:withHandler:). The second parameter, passed here with Swift's trailing closure syntax, is a closure that takes the data as an optional CMAccelerometerData instance, as well as an optional NSError. Inside the closure, which your motionManager will call on the motionQueue, you update the accelerometerData variable with the new data. Before using it, you'll need to make sure it's safe to access your accelerometer data from the main queue, where you'll need to read it for the UI.

Working with Data Across Multiple Queues

When you created the accelerometerData earlier, you started writing to it directly from the accelerometer update closure. These accelerometer updates all happen on the motionQueue you created. If you're writing to this variable on the motion queue while reading it from the main queue, bad things can happen. Let's serialize your access to this data so you can stay safe. You'll modify the declaration of accelerometerData to make it safer:

Chapter 11/Soccer/Soccer WatchKit Extension/InterfaceController.swift

```
Line 1  lazy var dataQueue = dispatch_queue_create("accelerometerData",
            DISPATCH_QUEUE_CONCURRENT)

  -     private var _accelerometerData = CMAcceleration(x: 0, y: 0, z: 0)
  5
  -     var accelerometerData: CMAcceleration
  -         {
  -         get {
  -             var data: CMAcceleration = CMAcceleration(x: 0, y: 0, z: 0)
 10
  -             dispatch_sync(dataQueue) {
  -                 data = self._accelerometerData
  -             }
  -
 15          return data
  -         }
```

```
        set {
            dispatch_barrier_async(dataQueue) {
                self._accelerometerData = newValue
            }
        }
    }
}
```

First, on line 1, you create another type of queue. Instead of an NSOperationQueue, you use dispatch_queue_create() to create a dispatch_queue_t instance. These queues, part of the Grand Central Dispatch APIs, are at a lower level than NSOperationQueue and will give you more control over how the queue is accessed. Next, on line 4, you create a private variable to store the accelerometer data. You'll use this variable to store the actual data but use the accelerometerData variable *without* the underscore to access it.

To actually access the data inside the get() for accelerometerData, you call dispatch_sync() on line 11. This method executes the closure passed to it on the given queue, waiting to return until the closure finishes. Since you created the queue with the DISPATCH_QUEUE_CONCURRENT attribute, multiple closures can execute at once; that's OK here because you're not modifying the value of _accelerometerData, just reading it. When you want to write to it in the set() method on line 18, you instead call dispatch_barrier_async(). The "async" portion of the method means that this returns immediately—the caller of the setter does not need to wait for it to finish. The "barrier" portion is what makes this safe—instead of running concurrently while other methods are reading the data, this method causes the queue to finish all closures sent to it before the barrier, execute *just* the barrier closure, and then resume normal operations. In this way, you can guarantee that nothing will read your data while you're writing to it but still allow for concurrent reads for things to be quick. This is a great general-purpose method of ensuring thread safety while still maintaining speed. Now that you've implemented it, you can put these values to use in the app's UI.

Moving Objects with Motion

Until now, you haven't looked at what's contained inside your accelerometerData; you've just stored it as is. The CMAccelerometerData class, of which accelerometerData is an instance, has only one property, acceleration, which itself is simply a struct called CMAcceleration. The CMAcceleration struct has three values: x, y, and z. These values measure the acceleration of the watch along three axes, relative to the pull of gravity. The X axis goes horizontally along the surface of the watch's screen, while the Y axis goes along the screen vertically. The Z axis goes perpendicular to the screen, coming out of it toward or away from you if you're looking at the watch. The values of the acceleration measure these axes. If the x value is 1.0, for instance, then that's indicative of a watch where the right side of the screen is facing down, because it's being pulled exactly 1 G toward the Earth. Using these values, you can track the acceleration of your ball. Since this is a cumulative effect, you'll store the ball's speed and then add to it or subtract from it as the user moves his watch. Let's add a variable for saving the speed:

Chapter 11/Soccer/Soccer WatchKit Extension/InterfaceController.swift

```
let maximumSpeed: Double = 5

var ballSpeed: (x: Double, y: Double) = (0, 0) {
    didSet {
        if ballSpeed.x > maximumSpeed {
            ballSpeed.x = maximumSpeed
        }

        if ballSpeed.x < -maximumSpeed {
            ballSpeed.x = -maximumSpeed
        }

        if ballSpeed.y > maximumSpeed {
            ballSpeed.y = maximumSpeed
        }

        if ballSpeed.y < -maximumSpeed {
            ballSpeed.y = -maximumSpeed
        }
    }
}
```

The maximumSpeed constant you defined ensures that the ball never moves too quickly; when you set the value of ballSpeed, you'll clamp it to that maximum value. A positive speed moves the ball to the right or down, whereas a negative speed moves the ball up or to the left. Next, you need to use these values in the UI. You'll be modifying the currentInsets property you created before, but you should add some additional logic to it to prevent the ball from leaving the screen:

Chapter 11/Soccer/Soccer WatchKit Extension/InterfaceController.swift

```
var currentInsets: UIEdgeInsets = UIEdgeInsetsZero {
    didSet {
        if currentInsets.left + ballSize.width > soccerFieldSize.width {
            currentInsets.left = soccerFieldSize.width - ballSize.width
        }

        if currentInsets.left < 0 {
            currentInsets.left = 0
        }
```

```
        if currentInsets.top + ballSize.height > soccerFieldSize.height {
            currentInsets.top = soccerFieldSize.height - ballSize.height
        }

        if currentInsets.top < 0 {
            currentInsets.top = 0
        }
    }
}
```

Now that you've done that, the ball will stay onscreen at all times. Perfect! It's time to use your updated data. You'll use an NSTimer to periodically update the ball's position. Create a new variable to store the timer:

Chapter 11/Soccer/Soccer WatchKit Extension/InterfaceController.swift

```
var updateTimer: NSTimer?
```

Next, at the end of the didAppear() method, you'll create the timer, having it run 30 times per second:

Chapter 11/Soccer/Soccer WatchKit Extension/InterfaceController.swift

```
if updateTimer == nil {
    updateTimer = NSTimer.scheduledTimerWithTimeInterval(1.0 / 30.0,
        target: self,
        selector: "updateAccelerometerData:",
        userInfo: nil,
        repeats: true)
}
```

When the timer runs, it will call a method named updateAccelerometerData(_:), so let's write that next:

Chapter 11/Soccer/Soccer WatchKit Extension/InterfaceController.swift

```
func updateAccelerometerData(timer: NSTimer) {
    let data = accelerometerData

    ballSpeed.x += data.x
    ballSpeed.y += -data.y

    currentInsets.left += CGFloat(ballSpeed.x)
    currentInsets.top += CGFloat(ballSpeed.y)

    soccerField.setContentInset(currentInsets)
}
```

This method applies the acceleration data from the accelerometer to the ball's speed, speeding it up or slowing it down depending on the watch's orientation. It then moves the ball according to its speed, repositioning it using the content inset of the soccer field, just as you had before. If you build and run the app on a watch device, you can move the ball around by moving your wrist!

(Accelerometer data is not available on the watchOS simulator, so this sample must be run on a watch device.) Now that you can do that, you can eliminate the buttons in the UI. Open the storyboard and delete the buttons, making the field fill the screen vertically by setting its height to 1 relative to its container. Update the soccerFieldSize variable to return the entire screen:

Chapter 11/Soccer/Soccer WatchKit Extension/InterfaceController.swift

```
var soccerFieldSize: CGSize {
    return contentFrame.size
}
```

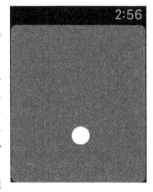

Build and run, and you'll see the soccer field alone, with the ball moving around inside it, as shown in the figure.

Using the accelerometer data in this way opens up a new realm of possibilities for your apps. Whether you create a system for using the Apple Watch as a three-dimensional remote control, integrate it into a workout app, or just use the data to see how your user moves around, sensor data is a great resource. Hopefully, future versions of the Apple Watch will include new sensors, giving you even more accurate device positioning. Next, let's look at another way the user's motion can influence your app: starting workouts with HealthKit!

Working Out with HealthKit

The sensors we looked at accessing in the previous part of this chapter, such as the accelerometer, are great at providing data about the device, but the Apple Watch has another sensor available to us that's *only* available on the watch: the heart rate sensor on the back of the device. This sensor, combined with the impressive water resistance of the watch, makes it an amazing companion for working out, whether you're a weekend warrior or professional athlete. Let's add support for this sensor to TapALap. You'll use the watch to save a *workout session* to HealthKit, which will allow you not only to access heart rate and calorie burn data but also to save the data back to the user's phone and contribute to his daily Activity rings!

What Is HealthKit?

One of Apple's main focuses with the Apple Watch is *health*. The device focuses much of its capability on its wearers' personal health: periodically sampling their heart rate, reminding users to stand periodically throughout the day, and encouraging them to make healthy habits like exercising for 30 minutes every day. To do these things, the watch needs a place to store the users' health data: heart rate readings, hours in which they've stood, and the exercise they've logged. These are all separate apps, too; the Workout app tracks workouts, the Activity app tracks standing, and so on. Wouldn't it be nice to share that data between apps?

HealthKit is Apple's answer to this set of needs. Instead of every health-related app creating its own system to store, synchronize, and share data, quickly leading to dozens of conflicting standards, Apple offers HealthKit as a common system framework to store personal health data. Apps can save health data to HealthKit, read data from HealthKit—even from other apps—and trust that the data is safe and secure on the user's device. Apps can use as much or as little of HealthKit as they want, but even an app that just saves user data to it makes the entire system more valuable to the user. Not only does HealthKit help you build your app by giving you a head start on your data store, but it can also serve to market your app. A user who's heavily invested in using HealthKit, when given the choice between two apps to do the same thing, one of which supports HealthKit and one of which doesn't, will choose the HealthKit app just to get his data in one place. Supporting HealthKit is a feature unto itself, but as you'll see in this chapter, it's also very handy when developing a workout app!

Whereas HealthKit is the interface we developers use to store health-related data, our users will use Apple's Health app on their iPhone to see a dashboard of their health data. In addition to the Health app, there's an Activity app to track the user's Apple Watch–specific activity: workout minutes, calories burned, and hours in which the user has stood. As you'll see later on page 165, supporting HealthKit will add your app to these apps, presenting your data in context for the user next to theirs. For more information on the Health and Activity apps, consult Apple's websites, both for iOS[1] and for watchOS.[2]

Asking for Permission

One of the biggest features of HealthKit is privacy. It's your users' most personal data, so Apple goes to great lengths to protect it. To that end, you can't just start writing code to talk to HealthKit; you need to ask the user if it's OK to proceed. The appropriate time to start saving data is when the user taps Start Run, so you'll ask the user for permission in the willActivate() method of

---

1. https://www.apple.com/ios/health/
2. https://www.apple.com/watch/health-and-fitness/

your RunTimerInterfaceController. First, you'll need to import the HealthKit framework to have access to the classes and methods you'll need:

Chapter 11/TapALap/TapALap WatchKit Extension/RunTimerInterfaceController.swift

```
import HealthKit
```

You'll need a lazy HKHealthStore to facilitate communication with HealthKit:

Chapter 11/TapALap/TapALap WatchKit Extension/RunTimerInterfaceController.swift

```
lazy var healthStore = HKHealthStore()
```

With that done, you can add a new method to your class, askForHealthKitPermission(), in which you'll actually ask the user for the permission you need. You'll call it from willActivate():

Chapter 11/TapALap/TapALap WatchKit Extension/RunTimerInterfaceController.swift

```
override func willActivate() {
    super.willActivate()

➤   askForHealthKitPermission()

    // Don't delete the rest of this method—it's just removed to save space!

}

func askForHealthKitPermission() {
    guard HKHealthStore.isHealthDataAvailable() else { return }

    guard let caloriesBurnedType = HKObjectType.quantityTypeForIdentifier(
        HKQuantityTypeIdentifierActiveEnergyBurned),
        distanceRunType = HKObjectType.quantityTypeForIdentifier(
            HKQuantityTypeIdentifierDistanceWalkingRunning) else { return }

    let shareTypes = Set([HKObjectType.workoutType(), caloriesBurnedType,
        distanceRunType])

    let readTypes = Set([caloriesBurnedType])

    healthStore.requestAuthorizationToShareTypes(shareTypes,
        readTypes: readTypes,
        completion: { (success: Bool, error: NSError?) in
            if let error = error where !success {
                print("Error authorizing HealthKit: " +
                    error.localizedDescription + ".")
            }
            else if !success {
                print("You didn't authorize HealthKit. Open the Health app on "
                    + "your iPhone to give TapALap the correct permissions.")
            }
    })
}
```

Before you do anything else, you call isHealthDataAvailable() to make sure that you can use HealthKit at all. If not, you simply return and do nothing. Next, you need to use some data types from HealthKit, but the methods to obtain them return optional types, so you use another guard statement to ensure they exist. You need data types for calories burned and the distance the user has run. Data types in hand, you need to tell HealthKit which data types you're reading and which you're writing—or, in the parlance of HealthKit, *sharing.* You want to share three pieces of data: workouts themselves, calories burned (which you'll associate with the workout later), and distance run. You put those in an array and then turn it into a Set, which is what HealthKit is expecting, called shareTypes. You need to do the same for the types you'll be reading from HealthKit. For now, you just need to read the calories burned, so it's the lone data type in your readTypes set. Armed with both Sets of types, you can call requestAuthorizationToShareTypes(_:readTypes:completion:). If this is the first time the app has run, the user will see an authentication dialog, allowing him to grant the app access.

The user won't actually give you permission on the watch, however. Instead, you need to open the iOS app delegate, where you're given a chance to perform the authorization. In the TapALap group, open AppDelegate.swift, import HealthKit, and add the following method:

Chapter 11/TapALap/TapALap/AppDelegate.swift

```
import HealthKit
```

Chapter 11/TapALap/TapALap/AppDelegate.swift

```
func applicationShouldRequestHealthAuthorization(application: UIApplication) {
    let store = HKHealthStore()

    store.handleAuthorizationForExtensionWithCompletion { success, error in
        if let error = error where !success {
            print("HealthKit authorization failed. Error: "
                + error.localizedDescription)
        }
    }
}
```

Now, when the extension requests HealthKit access, it'll get permission from the user by opening the iOS app as seen in the figures on page 155.

When the user taps Allow, your app will be granted access! For this to work, you just need to ensure that the WatchKit extension and iOS app have the HealthKit entitlement enabled in their app IDs.

With your HealthKit authorization complete, begin collecting your data.

Creating a Workout Session

At the core of your interaction with HealthKit is an HKWorkoutSession. Starting a workout session does a couple of things for you. Most importantly, it activates the heart rate sensor. Obviously, this will have an impact on your users' battery life, so you should only use a workout session for when the user is actually working out. Trying to use a workout session to see the user's heart rate while he sleeps at night, for example, would result in depleted batteries and sad users. Another benefit of creating a workout session, aside from the heart rate data, is that the watch will keep your app in the foreground automatically. The watch's screen will still turn off to conserve power, but when the user raises his wrist, the app with the foreground workout session will be visible instead of the watch face.

 Joe asks:

What is an entitlement, and how do I add one for HealthKit?

Much like a provisioning profile declares who can digitally sign your code and on which devices it can run, *entitlements* declare what the app is allowed to *do*. One of the most common entitlements is called get-task-allow, which allows the debugger to attach to release builds. Entitlements are specified in a property list file (typically Entitlements.plist) in your app, with the name of the entitlement as a string key and the associated Boolean value determining if your app supports that entitlement.

For any app to access HealthKit, add the HealthKit entitlement, com.apple.developer.healthkit, to its app ID. The easiest way to do this is using Xcode. Select the project settings, and then navigate to the Capabilities tab with TapALap WatchKit Extension selected. Click the switch next to HealthKit to enable it...*most* of the time.

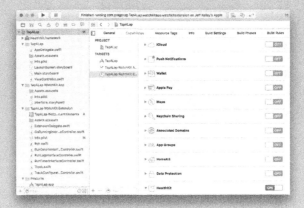

There are situations where the switch won't work to automatically enable the HealthKit entitlement. If that happens, you'll need to head to the developer center at https://developer.apple.com and enable it manually. Navigate to the Certificates, Identifiers, and Profiles section; then click App IDs. Select your app ID; then check the box next to HealthKit, as shown here:

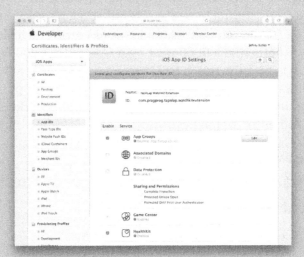

If you're doing this manually, you'll need to regenerate your provisioning profiles to include the new entitlement.

As you transition to the Run Timer interface controller and begin the run, you'll also start a workout session. To begin, you need to declare that the RunTimerInterfaceController conforms to the HKWorkoutSessionDelegate protocol. This will allow you to receive messages from the workout session as it's in progress:

Chapter 11/TapALap/TapALap WatchKit Extension/RunTimerInterfaceController.swift

```
class RunTimerInterfaceController: WKInterfaceController, HKWorkoutSessionDelegate {
```

Now it's time to actually start your workout session. You'll make a new method, startWorkoutSession(), in the interface controller:

Chapter 11/TapALap/TapALap WatchKit Extension/RunTimerInterfaceController.swift

```
var currentWorkoutSession: HKWorkoutSession?

func startWorkoutSession() {
    let session = HKWorkoutSession(activityType: .Running,
        locationType: .Indoor)

    session.delegate = self

    currentWorkoutSession = session

    healthStore.startWorkoutSession(session)
}
```

This method is a simple matter of creating a session, setting the interface controller as its delegate, and telling the health store to start the session. You'll use the currentWorkoutSession variable to keep track of it elsewhere. You provide a couple of options to the session, indicating that the workout is a run and it's taking place inside; then you're good to go. For it to be the session's delegate, however, you have to implement a pair of methods. First, and most simply, you have to implement workoutSession(_:didFailWithError:) to handle failure of the session:

Chapter 11/TapALap/TapALap WatchKit Extension/RunTimerInterfaceController.swift

```
func workoutSession(workoutSession: HKWorkoutSession,
    didFailWithError error: NSError) {
        print("Workout session error: \(error.localizedDescription)")
}
```

In this case, the workout session failing isn't the end of the world—you can still finish your run, add more laps, and so on, so you'll fail gracefully here, merely logging the error and continuing. Next, you'll need to implement workoutSession(_:didChangeToState:fromState:date:) to handle the workout ending:

Chapter 11/TapALap/TapALap WatchKit Extension/RunTimerInterfaceController.swift

```
func workoutSession(workoutSession: HKWorkoutSession,
    didChangeToState toState: HKWorkoutSessionState,
    fromState: HKWorkoutSessionState,
    date: NSDate) {
        // If the workout ends before we call endRun(), end the run.
        if let _ = lapTimes, _ = startDate where toState == .Ended {
            endRun()
        }
}
```

In this method, if the workout is changing to the Ended state, you call endRun().
Ending the workout session is as easy as starting it, so let's do that next.

Ending the Workout

With your delegate methods implemented, go to the endRun() method and end
your workout session:

Chapter 11/TapALap/TapALap WatchKit Extension/RunTimerInterfaceController.swift

```
func endRun() {
➤    if let session = currentWorkoutSession {
➤        healthStore.endWorkoutSession(session)
➤        currentWorkoutSession = nil
➤    }

    let names = ["GoRunning", "RunLog"]

    let contexts: [AnyObject]?

    if let lapTimes = lapTimes, startDate = startDate {
        let distance = track.lapDistance * Double(lapTimes.count)

        let run = Run(distance: distance,
            laps: lapTimes,
            startDate: startDate)

        let userDefaults = NSUserDefaults.standardUserDefaults()
        userDefaults.removeObjectForKey("LapTimes")
        userDefaults.removeObjectForKey("StartDate")
        userDefaults.synchronize()

        contexts = [NSNull(), run]
    }
    else {
        contexts = nil
    }

    WKInterfaceController.reloadRootControllersWithNames(names,
        contexts: contexts)
}
```

The lines at the top are enough to end the workout session. Easy, huh?
Calling endWorkoutSession(_:) on the HKHealthStore object is enough to save your

data, turn off the heart rate sensor, and allow other apps into the foreground of the watch. You're not quite finished yet, however; to allow your app to contribute to the user's Activity rings, you'll need to create an HKWorkout object to store all of this data in HealthKit.

Contributing to Activity Rings

So far what you've done has been sufficient for starting the heart rate monitor and keeping your app in the foreground. To make a workout app really shine, you need to use the data you're gathering as the user works out to contribute to his Activity rings in the Activity app on watchOS. These rings serve as motivation to work out, so by contributing to them, they will also serve as motivation to use your app! All you need to do is to save the workout to the watch when you're finished. You'll add a new method, saveWorkoutSession(_:), and call it after you end the workout session in endRun():

Chapter 11/TapALap/TapALap WatchKit Extension/RunTimerInterfaceController.swift

```
if let session = currentWorkoutSession {
    healthStore.endWorkoutSession(session)
    saveWorkoutSession(session)
    currentWorkoutSession = nil
}
```

The saveWorkoutSession(_:) method is responsible for creating an HKWorkout instance and saving it to HealthKit:

Chapter 11/TapALap/TapALap WatchKit Extension/RunTimerInterfaceController.swift

```
var currentCaloriesBurned = HKQuantity(unit: HKUnit.kilocalorieUnit(),
    doubleValue: 0.0)

var calorieSamples: [HKQuantitySample] = []

func saveWorkoutSession(session: HKWorkoutSession) {
    guard let caloriesBurnedType = HKObjectType.quantityTypeForIdentifier(
        HKQuantityTypeIdentifierActiveEnergyBurned),
        distanceRunType = HKObjectType.quantityTypeForIdentifier(
            HKQuantityTypeIdentifierDistanceWalkingRunning) else { return }

    // Ensure we have permission to save all types
    for type in [caloriesBurnedType, distanceRunType, .workoutType()] {
        if healthStore.authorizationStatusForType(type) != .SharingAuthorized {
            return
        }
    }

    guard let startDate = startDate, lapTimes = lapTimes
        where !lapTimes.isEmpty
        else { return }

    let endDate = startDate.dateByAddingTimeInterval(
```

❶ ❷ ❸ ❹

```
            lapTimes.reduce(0, combine: +))

        let lapDistance = track.lapDistance
⑤      let distanceRun = HKQuantity(unit: HKUnit.meterUnit(),
            doubleValue: lapDistance * Double(lapTimes.count))

⑥      let workout = HKWorkout(activityType: HKWorkoutActivityType.Running,
            startDate: startDate,
            endDate: endDate,
            duration: endDate.timeIntervalSinceDate(startDate),
            totalEnergyBurned: currentCaloriesBurned,
            totalDistance: distanceRun,
            metadata: nil)

⑦      let finalCalorieSamples = calorieSamples
⑧      healthStore.saveObject(workout) { [unowned self] success, error in
            if let error = error where !success {
                print("Failed to save the workout: "
                    + error.localizedDescription)
                return
            }

            if success && finalCalorieSamples.count > 0 {
                // Associate the accumulated samples with the workout.
⑨              self.healthStore.addSamples(finalCalorieSamples,
                    toWorkout: workout) { success, error in
                        if let error = error where !success {
                            print("Failed to add calorie samples to the workout:"
                                + error.localizedDescription)
                        }
                }
            }
        }

        if success {
            let lapDistanceQuantity = HKQuantity(unit: HKUnit.meterUnit(),
                doubleValue: lapDistance)

            var lapStartDate = startDate

            var samples: [HKSample] = []

⑩          for i in lapTimes.startIndex ..< lapTimes.endIndex {
                let lapTime = lapTimes[i]
                let lapEndDate = lapStartDate.dateByAddingTimeInterval(lapTime)

⑪              let sample = HKQuantitySample(type: distanceRunType,
                    quantity: lapDistanceQuantity,
                    startDate: lapStartDate,
                    endDate: lapEndDate,
                    device: HKDevice.localDevice(),
                    metadata: nil)

                samples.append(sample)

                lapStartDate = lapEndDate
```

```
            }
⑫      self.healthStore.addSamples(samples, toWorkout: workout)
             { success, error in
                 if let error = error where !success {
                     print("Failed to add distance samples to the workout:"
                         + error.localizedDescription)
                 }
             }
        }
      }
    }
}
```

There's a lot going on in this code sample. Let's go through it step-by-step:

❶ First, you need to create the required type objects that you'll use in HealthKit. Since these are optional values, you'll just exit early if you can't get them. Assuming you can, you should also have received permission to share them earlier when you asked the user for permission. You check each permission (at ❷) and exit early if any are incorrect.

❸ You need to get some required information about the workout, its start and end date. Here you get the array of lap times (ensuring that there's at least one lap), and from there you can compute the end date (at ❹).

❺ Since every lap is the same distance, you can multiply the track length by the number of laps to create the next value you'll need, an HKQuantity representing the number of meters the user ran.

❻ Finally, you're ready to create your HKWorkout. Its initializer takes all of the data you computed and returns the workout object itself.

❽ Now that you have a workout, you save it to your HKHealthStore. You aren't finished yet, because you still need to save the calorie data to it. You pass a closure to saveObject(_:completion:) that's called when the workout is saved and it's safe for you to add samples to it, so before you call the method (at ❼) you save a copy of the data into a local variable, ensuring that it won't be modified before the closure finishes running.

❾ Assuming the workout saved successfully, there are two sets of samples to add. First, you add the calories burned samples to the workout.

❿ Next, you add samples for how far the user ran. You know the distance of each lap, so you enumerate the lap times, creating HKQuantitySample objects (at ⑪) for each lap. The more you can give to HealthKit, the better.

⑫ Finally, you take these distance samples and add *them* to the workout. Having added all of the data, you're finished!

The steps we covered create the workout, save associated data to it, and store it in HealthKit. This is great for your users—this data can be shared with all kinds of apps, from weight loss apps to other running apps. Your users might want to use your app on rainy days where they run at the gym but use other apps for running outside, for instance. By implementing HealthKit, you make it easy to add your app to their existing workout regimen or create an entirely new one around it!

You may have noticed that the first two lines of the code sample were declaring variables that you read but never wrote to. You actually aren't *quite* finished; you created an empty array to store calorie burn samples and created your running "calories burned" total at 0, but you don't read that data anywhere. Next, we'll cover reading that data as it comes in from HealthKit so that you can save the information with the workout—and display it to your users onscreen!

Reading Calorie Burn Data

We know that starting a workout session on the watch will activate the heart rate sensor and start collecting data. What good is that if we don't use it? One of the coolest things it does is help to provide more accurate data during exercise. To that end, let's display the user's current calories burned on the Run Timer screen and also save the samples with the workout so they show up in the user's Activity rings.

First, open the TapALap watch app's Interface.storyboard and add a new label to the Run Timer interface controller with the text "Calories Burned:", as shown in the figure.

This label will need to fit the calories as well, so set its Minimum Font Scale to 0.5. Next, create a new @IBOutlet declaration in RunTimerInterfaceController.swift:

Chapter 11/TapALap/TapALap WatchKit Extension/RunTimerInterfaceController.swift

```
@IBOutlet weak var caloriesBurnedLabel: WKInterfaceLabel!
```

Finally, return to the storyboard and link them up. Now you're ready to start collecting data! You'll create a HealthKit *query* to instruct HealthKit to continuously deliver calorie data to you, rather than you having to continually ask it for updates. The right time to start this query is when the workout transitions to the running state. Add an else clause to the if in workoutSession(_:didChangeToState:fromState:date:) to handle this case:

Chapter 11/TapALap/TapALap WatchKit Extension/RunTimerInterfaceController.swift

```
func workoutSession(workoutSession: HKWorkoutSession,
    didChangeToState toState: HKWorkoutSessionState,
    fromState: HKWorkoutSessionState,
    date: NSDate) {
        // If the workout ends before we call endRun(), end the run.
        if let _ = lapTimes, _ = startDate where toState == .Ended {
            endRun()
        }
        else if toState == .Running {
            beginCalorieQuery()
        }
}
```

This code calls the beginCalorieQuery() method, which you haven't written yet.
Let's do that next:

Chapter 11/TapALap/TapALap WatchKit Extension/RunTimerInterfaceController.swift

```
Line 1  var currentCaloriesBurnedQuery: HKQuery?

        func beginCalorieQuery() {
            guard let calorieType = HKObjectType
     5          .quantityTypeForIdentifier(HKQuantityTypeIdentifierActiveEnergyBurned)
                else { return }

            let calorieUnit = HKUnit.kilocalorieUnit()

    10      guard let startDate = startDate else { return }

            let datePredicate = HKQuery.predicateForSamplesWithStartDate(startDate,
                endDate: nil, options: .None)

    15      let processCalorieSamplesFromQuery = { (query: HKAnchoredObjectQuery,
                samples: [HKSample]?,
                deletedObjects: [HKDeletedObject]?,
                anchor: HKQueryAnchor?,
                error: NSError?) -> Void in
    20
                guard let samples = samples as? [HKQuantitySample] else { return }

                let newSamples = samples.map { originalSample in
                    HKQuantitySample(type: calorieType,
    25                  quantity: originalSample.quantity,
                        startDate: originalSample.startDate,
                        endDate: originalSample.endDate)
                }

    30          NSOperationQueue.mainQueue().addOperationWithBlock { [weak self] in
                    guard let initialCaloriesBurned = self?.currentCaloriesBurned
                        .doubleValueForUnit(calorieUnit) else { return }
```

```
       let newCaloriesBurned = samples.reduce(initialCaloriesBurned) {
35         $0 + $1.quantity.doubleValueForUnit(calorieUnit)
       }

       self?.currentCaloriesBurned = HKQuantity(unit: calorieUnit,
           doubleValue: newCaloriesBurned)
40
       self?.caloriesBurnedLabel
           .setText("Calories Burned: \(newCaloriesBurned)")

       self?.calorieSamples += newSamples
45   }
   }

   let query = HKAnchoredObjectQuery(type: calorieType,
       predicate: datePredicate,
50     anchor: nil,
       limit: Int(HKObjectQueryNoLimit),
       resultsHandler: processCalorieSamplesFromQuery)

   query.updateHandler = processCalorieSamplesFromQuery
55
   healthStore.executeQuery(query)

   currentCaloriesBurnedQuery = query
}
```

You start on line 1 by creating a variable to store your query in. You'll need
to reference this later when it's time to stop the query. Next, after getting your
prerequisite data on lines 4 through 10, you create a *predicate* on line 12 that
you'll use to filter the data. The predicate will restrict the search results to
just those that came in *after* the workout began—otherwise you'd start processing unrelated items! Next, on line 15, you create a closure called process-
CalorieSamplesFromQuery. You'll use this closure in two places to process results.
The samples parameter to the closure is an array of calorie burn samples. As
they come in, you create duplicates on line 23. This might seem weird, but
it's necessary to get the proper attribution—since your app created the new
samples, your app will "own" them and show up next to them in the Health
app on the user's phone.

Next, on line 30, you wrap the rest of the code in a closure that gets executed
on the main queue. Since you're going to be updating some more variables
and the UI from here, you want to make sure nothing happens out of order.
You use the [weak self] *capture list* to avoid the closure taking ownership of self
and causing a reference cycle. If the interface controller is deallocated before
the query stops processing, self will be nil when this closure executes and
nothing will happen.

Inside the closure, you first get the current calories burned and save it as initialCaloriesBurned. On line 34, use the reduce() method to add all of the samples' data to initialCaloriesBurned. After reducing your calories, create a new HKQuantity out of the new number and save it off. You update your new label with the new amount of calories burned; then on line 44 add the samples to your array of samples, which is what you'll save to the workout when it's saved.

After the closure, on line 48, it's time to create the query. You pass processCalorieSamplesFromQuery in as its resultsHandler and also set it as the query's updateHandler. The former is called as soon as the query starts with all of the existing data, and the latter is called whenever new data arrives. Since you need to do the same processing for existing and new data, the same closure works in each case. Finally, you instruct your healthStore to start the query and save it as your currentCaloriesBurnedQuery. All that's left is to stop it when you've finished.

To end the query, call stopQuery(_:) on your healthStore. Do this inside endRun():

Chapter 11/TapALap/TapALap WatchKit Extension/RunTimerInterfaceController.swift

```
func endRun() {
    if let query = currentCaloriesBurnedQuery {
        healthStore.stopQuery(query)
        currentCaloriesBurnedQuery = nil
    }

    // Don't delete the rest of this method, it's merely removed to save space!
}
```

And with that, you can start a run! You'll notice the calories updating live as you run, and when you end the run, your watch will automatically sync the data with the phone. TapALap will even appear in the iPhone's Activity app in the Move section, as shown here!

Wrap-Up

With the addition of HealthKit, TapALap is more useful than ever. In a short amount of time, we've opened up its data to a larger world of health apps. These apps are a great opportunity for developers to not only create great apps with lots of users but also effect real healthy change in lifestyles around the world. I encourage you to use HealthKit whenever possible in an app that records (or uses) health-related data.

You also learned how to use other sensors in your apps, and while only the accelerometer is currently available, it's enough to make some neat interfaces. Using HealthKit and sensor data in a watch app takes the interaction beyond the screen and into the real world.

None of this cool stuff matters, however, if your apps are so slow that your users won't want to use them. Next, let's look at some ways you can take an underperforming watch app and turn it into a shining example of big performance from a little device.

CHAPTER 12

Unlocking Watch App Performance

So far in this book, you've seen a lot of awesome features for the Apple Watch. None of them matter, however, unless your users want to keep using your app. An app that's slow or unresponsive is more likely to be abandoned by its users than one that responds quickly and always shows the user what it's doing. Good performance, aside from being faster for users, means your app will consume less energy.

In this chapter, we're going to look at some common performance pitfalls on watchOS and some ways that you can mitigate them in your own code to have the smooth, quick app your users expect. We'll also look at how Xcode's tools can help you pinpoint slow code and make it fast again.

Making Apps Launch Quickly

The most critical time for a watch app's performance is when it launches. While a watch app is loading, the system displays the loading indicator, shown here, and finally replaces it with the app's initial user interface. If an app takes too long to launch, the screen will go to sleep before it's even done, and the user may well forget they even launched it. It would be a pity if the loading indicator was the only part of your app that your users saw! To avoid this misfortune, let's look at each thing the app does when it starts and try to make it happen faster.

Efficient Interface Controller Loading

When a watch app loads, the interface controller marked as the initial interface controller is loaded and presented to the user. It needs to complete loading before the user can interact with it. All of the interface controller lifecycle methods need to finish: init(), awakeWithContext(_:), and willActivate(). You can test this yourself by adding logging to these methods; the logs will appear before the app loads.

It's easy for me to tell you to make these methods fast. The trouble is *how*? There are some watch-specific things you can do to make these methods faster. For instance, you can reduce the amount of data loaded by the storyboard. If your storyboard has a 10-megapixel image inside a button, the system has to load the *entire image*, shrink it down to the appropriate size, and then render it onscreen. If you use an appropriately sized image, the watch only has to load the image and render it.

Not only does the system load the initial interface controller at app launch time; it will also load any interface connected to it using a "next page" segue. If you have five interface controllers linked using "next page" segues, the first of which is marked as the initial interface controller, the system will call init() and awakeWithContext(_:) on *each* interface controller in turn. This compounds the performance implications of loading each interface controller. For instance, if they have tables with many items in them and the tables are initialized in awakeWithContext(_:), all of that initialization has to happen for each interface controller, even if the user will never navigate to some of them.

You might think that the solution to this problem is to avoid doing complicated initialization in init() and awakeWithContext(_:) in favor of using willActivate(), and you'd be partially correct. Moving data-intensive tasks like loading data into tables into willActivate() can help delay when the data is loaded. In the case of app startup, there's one important detail when it comes to paged interface controllers. Consider the following layout of interface controllers:

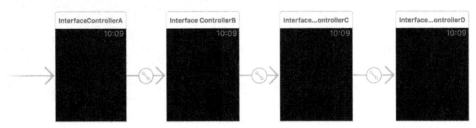

This sample app has four interface controllers, named InterfaceControllerA through InterfaceControllerD. They're all loaded at app startup as a group of paged interface controllers, and I've added logging to them to see the sequence of events at app startup. Here's the output from those logs:

```
InterfaceControllerA.init()
InterfaceControllerA.awakeWithContext(_:)
InterfaceControllerB.init()
InterfaceControllerB.awakeWithContext(_:)
InterfaceControllerC.init()
InterfaceControllerC.awakeWithContext(_:)
InterfaceControllerD.init()
InterfaceControllerD.awakeWithContext(_:)
InterfaceControllerA.willActivate()
InterfaceControllerB.willActivate()
InterfaceControllerB.didDeactivate()
```

Everything seems fine at first: the interface controllers are initialized with both init() and awakeWithContext(_:), and then InterfaceControllerA receives the willActivate() method. But what happens next is interesting: InterfaceControllerB receives willActivate() immediately followed by didDeactivate(). Why is that? If you swipe from one to the next, you'll see why. Here's the log output from swiping to the second interface controller:

```
InterfaceControllerB.willActivate()
InterfaceControllerA.didDeactivate()
InterfaceControllerC.willActivate()
InterfaceControllerC.didDeactivate()
```

As you swipe, InterfaceControllerB receives willActivate(), and InterfaceControllerA receives didDeactivate(). That seems fair and just, because you're leaving A to arrive at B. Next, you see the same oddity: InterfaceControllerC receives the willActivate() and didDeactivate() methods right after one another. Why is this? The answer is a performance trick on watchOS's part. By calling willActivate() on the interface controller, any work you need to do before the user swipes to an interface controller can be performed, and then you return to an inactive state in didDeactivate(). When the user swipes to the next interface controller, anything in willActivate() that needs to happen only once has already happened, so the swipe happens as quickly as possible. It's a performance trick that you should be aware of at app startup as well.

Efficient App Startup in the Extension Delegate

The initial interface controller in a watch app's storyboard isn't the only thing that needs to load before an app starts. The extension delegate lifecycle methods are also called before the loading indicator disappears, so it's paramount to return from them immediately. You can see the sequence of events by running a sample app with logging added. The app I have been referencing is available in the book's source code download, at code/Chapter 12/SlowLauncher. Running it shows that after the interface controllers initialize, two lifecycle methods fire: applicationDidFinishLaunching() followed by applicationDidBecomeActive().

There's nothing special to these methods in terms of performance, but there is an important caveat with applicationDidFinishLaunching(). In that method, you can call WKInterfaceController's reloadRootControllersWithNames(_:contexts:) method to load initial interface controllers other than those specified in the storyboard. However, this method happens *after* the storyboard's interface controllers are loaded, so if your storyboard has a complicated interface controller as its initial interface controller, and then you load another complicated interface controller in the extension delegate, you're wasting those resources. You can't just leave the initial interface controller unset in the storyboard, because this results in a build error. If you'd rather just load your initial interface controllers in the extension delegate, one trick to increase performance is to set the initial interface controller in your storyboard to an empty interface controller. At least you know it'll load quickly!

These methods can help the app start up more quickly and reduce the amount of time users see the dreaded loading indicator. App startup isn't the only time performance matters; there are things you can do throughout the app to increase responsiveness. Let's look at those next.

Increasing Performance by Removing Data

One of the examples earlier was loading complicated table data, which is something that can add complexity to an app as the amount of data in the table grows. Delaying until willActivate() to load data into the table buys you time, but you still need to load the data at some point. The best and easiest way to make this faster is to simply load fewer rows. Users aren't going to want to scroll through 10,000 rows on their watches using their finger or the Digital Crown *anyway*, so capping the total number of rows can go a long way toward making the app responsive. Another technique that can give the appearance of performance is to load part of the data first and then load the rest asynchronously afterward so it's there when the user scrolls. Let's implement this method in TapALap to help it remain as fast as possible.

Open up TapALap and head to RunLogInterfaceController.swift. You'll modify the willActivate() method to load five rows at a time:

```
override func willActivate() {
    super.willActivate()

    guard let runs = runs else { return }

    runTable.setNumberOfRows(max(runs.count, 5), withRowType: "RunRow")

    for i in 0 ..< runTable.numberOfRows {
        guard let rowController = runTable.rowControllerAtIndex(i)
            as? RunLogRowController else { continue }

        configureRow(rowController, forRun: runs[i])
    }

    if runs.count > 5 {
        var position = 5

        let groupsOfFiveRuns = 5.stride(to: runs.count, by: 5).map {
            Array(runs[$0..<$0.advancedBy(5, limit: runs.count)])
        }

        for next5runs in groupsOfFiveRuns {
            NSOperationQueue.mainQueue().addOperationWithBlock {
                let range = NSMakeRange(position, next5runs.count)

                self.runTable.insertRowsAtIndexes(
                    NSIndexSet(indexesInRange: range),
                    withRowType: "RunRow")

                for i in position ..< position + next5runs.count {
                    guard let rowController = self.runTable
                        .rowControllerAtIndex(i)
                        as? RunLogRowController else { continue }

                    self.configureRow(rowController,
                        forRun: next5runs[i - position])
                }

                position += range.length
            }
        }
    }
}
```

This code gets long, let's break it down. First, at line 6, you use only the first five runs when setting the initial data in the table. Configure those rows as you had before, and then if there are more runs, you iterate through them. Using stride(to:by:), you create a list of integers, which you then map(_:) over to create individual arrays of five runs each. The resulting variable, groupsOf-FiveRuns, is an array containing arrays of runs, each with up to five in it.

Once you have these arrays, use NSOperationQueue's addOperationWithBlock(_:) method on line 23 to delay adding it. These blocks are called on the main queue but *after* willActivate() has already returned, allowing the user to interact with the app while you're busy adding rows. Inside the block, add new rows to the table on line 26, configure them as usual, and you're good to go. This small improvement can make a huge difference in the loading speed of your app.

Inspecting Performance with Instruments

We've looked at a few places where you can make an app faster, but what about the rest of the time? How can you make a method return faster if you don't know where it's slow? You can guess, looking at the code with your brow furrowed until you decide to change something, but that's problematic. Not only could you be ignoring non-obvious performance problems, but in your attempt to fix the issue, you could actually make it slower!

What you need is *data*, and that's where *Instruments*, a performance-analysis and testing tool bundled with Xcode, comes in. Let's try it out.

In Xcode, open TapALap and select Product → Profile or press ⌘I. This builds your app in its *Release* configuration, which performs additional optimizations and is closer to what the final product in the App Store will be. It's important to perform those optimizations before profiling the code; otherwise, you might end up improving code that will be optimized anyway. Once the app is built, Instruments is launched and asks you to select an instrument from an array of profiling templates, shown in the following figure.

What you want is Time Profiler. Select that, and click Choose.

The window that appears next looks like a video editing interface. This is the main Instruments window and will display the processing in your app over time. Other instruments show things like memory allocation, memory leaks, and graphics processing over time. Time Profiler helps you understand where your code is taking the longest to run. First, you need to run the app. Click the red record button in the toolbar, and the app will launch. You'll see the app start in the simulator, but you'll also see data start coming in about the app's performance. After the app's startup process has finished and new data stops coming in, you can click the Stop button to quit the app. Now you can analyze the data that came in.

Since you're interested only in your own code, there are some boxes you can check to make navigation easier. Click the gear icon on the right-hand side or press ⌘2 to open Display Settings. Check Invert Call Tree and Hide System Libraries, and uncheck Separate By Thread. This will rearrange the code to be a bit friendlier to go through. Expanding the first element in the list will show you the longest running piece of code, shown here:

The real power of Instruments comes when you select the first element in the list and double-click it. The screen changes from the list of method calls to your code, annotated with how slow each individual line is. As you can see in the screenshot on page 174, three of the lines of code in the lower-left section have shaded backgrounds that correspond to how much time is spent on those particular lines. According to the data, we're spending a lot of time using distance formatters and duration formatters.

With this data in hand, you can run your app in Instruments, examine where it's slow, and try to fix it. In this case, you might try to cache the result of the distance and duration formatters to make it faster. The important thing about Instruments, however, is that you get *real* data out of it. Instead of poking around blindly, you can make actionable decisions about your code and see real results.

Time Profiler is but one of many amazing tools available in Instruments. You can use the Allocations instrument to view the history of every object allocated by your app, from creation to destruction. Use the Leaks instrument to analyze memory leaks and pinpoint the objects that are sticking around. You can even create custom instruments. If you want to track memory leaks while also using Time Profiler, it's as easy as dragging tools out of a library. For more information on Instruments, a great place to start is Apple's WWDC videos.[1]

Sometimes things are unavoidably slow, no matter how good your code is—such as loading things from the network on a slow hotel Wi-Fi connection. In those cases, how can you make your app fast? Let's look at one more technique: preloading data.

The Illusion of Performance: Preloading Data

No matter how fast your network connection, waiting for a request to finish, parsing the data, and then updating the UI takes time. On the watch, this is

---

1. https://developer.apple.com/videos/wwdc

time you don't have. The screen is going to turn off in a matter of seconds, and you need to be finished before then! One thing you can do to avoid frustrating your users with loading indicators is to load the data before they even get there. For that, the parent iOS app is your best friend.

One of the features of iOS that you can use in your iPhone app is Background Fetch.[2] It's a multitasking mode that will wake your app periodically to allow it to download new data. This is perfect for your needs! When you implement Background Fetch, you can *also* implement WatchConnectivity to send data to the watch app. In fact, anytime your iOS app loads data, whether it's in the background or the foreground, you should have it also send that data to the watch. WatchConnectivity will take care of when your watch app is actually called with the data, so don't be shy about sending it proactively. This is also a great time to refresh your complications' data.

An important step in preloading data is to determine how frequently your app actually needs to refresh its data. A weather app providing a forecast probably needs to refresh no more than once an hour, and a weather app providing current conditions might be okay with a fifteen-minute interval between updates. On the other hand, a sports app providing live scores needs to continually refresh (or receive updates via push notification). Once you've determined the appropriate interval for your app, it's important to *do nothing* when your app loads and you have new-enough data. If the user swipes over to your Glance and you have recent data, just display it. There's no need to create a new network request. Already having the data on hand can make your app feel instantaneous, no matter how slow the actual network request took. This kind of attention to detail can make all the difference for your user.

Wrap-Up

We've explored a number of ways to increase your app's performance in this chapter. Since time is so precious on Apple Watch, performance is paramount. Using these techniques and tools to boost your app's performance will result in happier users. They might not even notice that your app is performant, and that's the idea. You want your app to feel instantaneous so your users don't think about how long it's taking; instead they focus on what they're doing. In the next chapter, we'll look at another way you can endear your app to its users, by making them feel at home with their own language, their own units of measure, and support for any accessibility options they've enabled.

---

2. https://developer.apple.com/library/ios/documentation/iPhone/Conceptual/iPhoneOSProgrammingGuide/Back-groundExecution/BackgroundExecution.html

Being a Good Watch App Citizen

Our little app TapALap has grown into a pretty useful workout tool! Time to ship, right? Well, probably not. We want TapALap to be useful for as many people as possible, but so far we've been considering only a relatively small portion of our potential userbase: English-speaking people who live in the United States and don't have visual or other physical impairments. The signs of this are everywhere: our text is exclusively in the English language, our units are in miles, and we haven't even *thought* about what our app is like for a vision-impaired user. We're going to want to fix all of this before we ship. By supporting more languages, countries, and user capabilities, we'll open up our app to more potential users—it's just good business.

Localizing and Internationalizing Your App

So far, TapALap has been only in English. For a large app with a large customer base, you'll want to support multiple languages. Think of every new language you support as an entirely new market of users. The process of supporting multiple languages is *localization*, commonly abbreviated *L10n*. *Internationalization*, or *i18n* for short, is the similar process of adapting your app for different locales and cultures, going beyond the written word.

Localizing TapALap

To localize TapALap, first you need to tell Xcode that you intend to support another language. Open the project settings by clicking the top-level TapALap in Xcode's Project Navigator (⌘1). Select TapALap under Project, and then select the Info tab. Under Localizations, tap the + button to add a new localization. Select French, and Xcode will present a window with some options for localization. Keep them all selected and choose Finish. Great! Now you have French as a localization option, as shown in the figure on page 178. But how do you put in different words?

Localizing Storyboard Content

Look at Interface.storyboard in the Project Navigator, and notice a disclosure tri-
angle to its left. Selecting it reveals the Spanish version of the Interface.strings
file, which Xcode created to store the localized versions of all of the strings
in the storyboard. Open the file to see a list of all of the strings in the storyboard. If you replace the contents with their French versions, your French
users will automatically see the French text. Here are a couple of examples:

Chapter 13/TapALap/TapALap WatchKit App/fr.lproj/Interface.strings

```
/* Class = "WKInterfaceButton"; title = "Stop Run"; ObjectID = "0Fd-Oq-zqB"; */
"0Fd-Oq-zqB.title" = "Arrêter la course";

/* Class = "WKInterfaceLabel"; text = "Run Date"; ObjectID = "0Ta-W8-PXh"; */
"0Ta-W8-PXh.text" = "Date de la course";

/* Class = "WKInterfaceLabel"; text = "Lap"; ObjectID = "2OB-6V-MaP"; */
"2OB-6V-MaP.text" = "Tour";

/* Class = "WKInterfaceButton"; title = "Finish Lap"; ObjectID = "3AS-d7-yOK"; */
"3AS-d7-yOK.title" = "Finir le tour";
```

Getting Good Localized Content

For this example text, I used a professional service to translate
the app. You may be tempted to use an online tool such as Google
Translate to perform these translations for you, but be careful!
With it, at best your app will be an awkward, obviously machine-
generated translation, but at worst it will be mistranslated in a
way that generates offense or otherwise misses the mark for your
brand. In a real, shipping app, you'll want to use a translation
service to obtain actual translations of your text. These services
aren't wildly expensive compared to the potential upside of
reaching a new market of customers.

Before you ship your localized app, you'll want to see it running in another language, of course. Aside from running it on a device that's set to the target language, there are two ways to preview your localized edits. The first way is the Preview feature in Interface Builder to see the app running in two languages at the same time. Open Interface.storyboard and open the Assistant Editor with ⌘⌥↵. Open the Preview interface, and create two 42mm watches. Select one of them by clicking it, and then in the lower-right corner, click English and change it to French. You can now see both languages next to one another, as in the image here.

As you can see, there's already a problem: the text is too wide in a couple of places in French. This is where the preview earns its keep; as you tweak your UI to make things work, you see the results in all languages. (German is notorious for long words.) Once you've tweaked things to your liking, it's time to run the app in the iOS Simulator. Simply change the language in your iOS Simulator's Settings app to French, and you'll be able to see the changes as you run the app.

Joe asks:
How do I switch my simulator's language?

While you can certainly run your app on a real Apple Watch and set its language and region settings in the Settings app, managing the language that way is a hassle. The last thing you want is to be stuck trying to find the right area of the Settings app to change it back because you can't read anything! Fortunately, Xcode has a feature to help. An Xcode scheme can be set to run the app in a specific language or region. One good trick is to duplicate your main scheme and give it a language-specific name, then open the Edit Scheme window with ⌘<, select Run on the left, and then select the Options tab. Setting Application Language and Application Region, as you can see in the screenshot on page 180, will run the app with the given settings. Try it out!

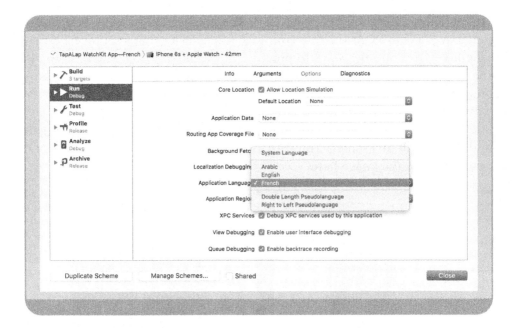

Localizing Textual Content

Not every piece of text in your app lives in the storyboard. For text that you use in code, you'll use another strings file. In Xcode, select File → New → File…, and select Strings File under Resource in the watchOS section on the left. Name the file Localizable.strings and make sure it's added to the WatchKit extension. This file will have multiple versions, one per language, but it starts with just an English version. To add another version, open the file and head to the Identity Inspector (⌘⌥1). Under Localization, click Localize… and select Localize from the resulting dialog. Now, under the Identity Inspector, you can select the languages you'd like to localize.

The Localizable.strings file has the same format as the storyboard's strings file, albeit without some of the extra storyboard data. Add a French version and add a few translations:

Chapter 13/TapALap/TapALap WatchKit Extension/fr.lproj/Localizable.strings

```
"Error" = "Erreur";

"You need to select a track to run on!" =
        "Vous devez sélectionner une piste sur laquelle courir !";

"OK" = "OK";

"None" = "Aucun";
```

Now, in order to use these strings in code, you need to read this file. Open GoRunningInterfaceController.swift to make the modifications. First, you modify the Selected Track button—if no track is selected, you use the text "None" for its name. Let's localize that string using NSLocalizedString(_:comment:), which pulls the correct text out of the app bundle:

Chapter 13/TapALap/TapALap WatchKit Extension/GoRunningInterfaceController.swift

```
func updateTrackLabels() {
    if let track = selectedTrack {
        trackNameLabel.setText(track.name)

        trackDistanceLabel.setText(
            distanceFormatter.stringFromMeters(track.lapDistance))
    }
    else {
➤       trackNameLabel.setText(NSLocalizedString("None", comment: ""))
        trackDistanceLabel.setText(nil)
    }
}
```

Next up, you handle the error message that appears when you try to start a run with no track selected:

Chapter 13/TapALap/TapALap WatchKit Extension/GoRunningInterfaceController.swift

```
@IBAction func startRunButtonPressed() {
    guard let track = selectedTrack else {
➤       presentAlertControllerWithTitle(NSLocalizedString("Error", comment: ""),
➤           message: NSLocalizedString("You need to select a track to run on!",
➤               comment: ""),
➤           preferredStyle: .Alert,
➤           actions: [
➤               WKAlertAction(title: NSLocalizedString("OK", comment: ""),
➤                   style: .Default,
➤                   handler: {})
➤           ])

        return
    }

    let names = ["RunTimer"]

    WKInterfaceController.reloadRootControllersWithNames(names,
        contexts: [track])
}
```

Here, you grab two more strings out of the file to use in your interface. If you run the app with your simulator's language set to French, you'll see the translation in action as shown in the screenshot on page 182.

Just like that, your code for this screen is ready. If NSLocalizedString(_:comment:) doesn't find what it's looking for in French—or whatever language the watch is set to—it'll fall back to your English version. Between localized strings files and storyboards, it's actually pretty simple to support multiple languages. The only confusing part comes when it's time to support the right-to-left languages.

Supporting Right-to-Left Languages

As of watchOS 2.1, the platform fully supports right-to-left languages. What does this mean for us as developers? While not as straightforward as supporting multiple left-to-right languages, it's actually much easier than you might think! When you add a right-to-left language, your user interface flips horizontally to match. This is why instead of "left" and "right" for some interface values, iOS and watchOS use "leading" and "trailing." For right-to-left languages, "leading" is on the right, not the left!

To control what happens to an interface object, use the setSemanticContentAttribute(_:) method. Passing in values like .ForceLeftToRight helps watchOS to determine your intent. Most of the time, you'll want your objects to flip, but if you have something that's purely directional—like our soccer ball example from earlier in this book—it might make sense to force a specific orientation.

For images, you can use UIImage's imageFlippedForRightToLeftLayoutDirection() method to flip an image, but only for right-to-left layouts. Between these two methods, supporting right-to-left languages like Arabic and Hebrew is actually fairly easy! As you can see in this Arabic screenshot, TapALap looks great in either direction.

Localization makes a dramatic impact on your app and opens it to customers you could never have hoped to reach with a single language. It does bring with it a bit of a support burden: once you ship your app with a language, you should be prepared to receive support emails in that language.

Internationalizing Your App

Like localization, internationalization expands your app's reach to a new set of users, but it does so in a much subtler way. Instead of translating the user-interface text, internationalization covers tasks such as using metric units rather than imperial, using the proper date format, and placing events in your users' time zones. Unlike localization, you can do much of this work yourself, using built-in system classes.

Of all the nice things in Apple's frameworks, you have been using some of the nicest and didn't even know it. Remember how you used NSDateFormatter and NSLengthFormatter earlier? Well, guess what? Those classes are already internationalized right out of the box. When using NSDateFormatter to format a date, you get the date formatted in the user's current locale. 12/25/2016 might be Christmas 2016 in America, but in France that's written as 25/12/2016, and if you use NSDateFormatter to do your formatting, you won't have to write even a single line of code to get it right. Similarly, NSLengthFormatter will show the optimal unit for the distance given the user's locale. Other system-provided NSFormatter subclasses also take the user's locale into account, meaning that for most cases where you want to display data to the user, an NSFormatter is the way to go.

Sometimes you need to do some internationalization yourself. In TapALap, you will do this on the track configuration screen. To determine if you should show miles or kilometers, you'll use NSLocale. By using NSLocale's NSLocaleUsesMetricSystem key, you let the system control which unit of measure you're using. There are many keys that you can use with NSLocale; read the class documentation for a full list. You encapsulate this key in a lazy property so you need to read it only once. Open TrackConfigurationInterfaceController.swift and add a new property:

```
lazy var usesMetric: Bool = {
    return NSLocale.currentLocale()
        .objectForKey(NSLocaleUsesMetricSystem) as? Bool ?? false
}()
```

Now that you have usesMetric, you can determine if you ought to display distance units in miles or kilometers. Modify awakeWithContext(_:) to use this value:

```
override func awakeWithContext(context: AnyObject?) {
    super.awakeWithContext(context)

    if let receiver = context as? TrackSelectionReceiver {
        self.trackReceiver = receiver
    }

    // Add 1-10 laps for laps picker
    let lapItems: [WKPickerItem] = (1 ... 10).map { i in
        let pickerItem = WKPickerItem()
        pickerItem.title = "\(i)"
        pickerItem.caption = (i == 1) ? "Lap" : "Laps"
        return pickerItem
    }

    lapsPicker.setItems(lapItems)

    // Add 0.5 - 5 miles for total distance picker
    var distanceItems: [WKPickerItem] = []

    let distanceFormatter = NSLengthFormatter()
    distanceFormatter.numberFormatter.minimumFractionDigits = 1
    distanceFormatter.numberFormatter.maximumFractionDigits = 1

    for i in 0.5.stride(to: 5.5, by:0.5) {
        let pickerItem = WKPickerItem()

        if usesMetric {
            pickerItem.title = distanceFormatter.stringFromValue(i,
                unit: .Kilometer)
        }
        else {
            pickerItem.title = distanceFormatter.stringFromValue(i,
                unit: .Mile)
        }

        distanceItems.append(pickerItem)
    }

    distancePicker.setItems(distanceItems)

    // Set values based on initial picker values.
    lapsPickerDidChange(selectedIndex: 0)
    distancePickerDidChange(selectedIndex: 0)
}
```

You aren't changing the values used, just whether they represent miles or kilometers. To change the values, you need to modify distancePickerDidChange(selectedIndex:) to also inspect the value of usesMetric:

Chapter 13/TapALap/TapALap WatchKit Extension/TrackConfigurationInterfaceController.swift

```swift
@IBAction func distancePickerDidChange(selectedIndex i: Int) {
    if usesMetric {
        selectedDistance = Double(i + 1) / 2.0 * 1000
    }
    else {
        // Convert from miles to meters
        selectedDistance = Double(i + 1) / 2.0 * 1609.34
    }
}
```

Build and run on a watch set to a region that uses the metric system, and you'll see the units are now in kilometers:

You're finished! TapALap will now automatically work for people who live in countries that use the metric system. As you can see, internationalization can be complicated, but it will pay off in spades because users from all over the globe have access to your app.

Internationalization and localization are two sides to the same coin. Consider them features of your app: all users can feel at home, like the app was made for just them. To do it right, every piece of text that your users see should be localized, and every non-text string that you present—be it a formatted date, a number, or even the style of quotation marks—should be internationalized. Sure, it's a lot of work for you, but with an app that supports every language in the App Store and is properly internationalized, you can consider the entire iOS user base as potential customers, and that's extremely powerful.

Supporting Every User with Accessibility

One of the most amazing things about the Apple Watch is how useful it is for people with disabilities. Much like the iPhone, you might think that a person with visual impairment would have serious difficulty using it. Even someone who has trouble reading small text would have difficulty with Apple Watch—it's a small piece of glass (or sapphire) with no buttons on the surface and tiny text. However, watchOS includes some amazing accessibility features to help these users and others. From simple things, like making the text bigger onscreen or zooming in to the entire interface, to larger affordances like VoiceOver, which speaks the items onscreen using text-to-speech, the accessibility features of watchOS make the device great for a much wider range of users. The best part is that for us developers, supporting these features in our apps is incredibly simple and straightforward. Really, the only feature we need to do anything to support is VoiceOver.

Setting Up VoiceOver

There are a few ways to set up VoiceOver on an Apple Watch. You can open the watchOS Settings app, navigate to General, then Accessibility, then VoiceOver, and turn it on manually. Or, you can do the same in the iPhone Apple Watch Settings app. For development purposes, you're probably going to want to turn it on and off a lot. For that, the easiest way is to open the Watch iPhone companion app and navigate to Accessibility under General. Tap Accessibility Shortcut and then VoiceOver. This will enable triple-clicking the Digital Crown on your watch to toggle VoiceOver's activation state. For debugging your app's accessibility support, this is by far the most convenient option.

The rest of this chapter will focus on VoiceOver support, but while you're enabling VoiceOver to test your app, check out the other accessibility features that are available. Even better—enable them; then start your app. Start some other apps on your watch. You'll quickly realize a difference between apps that support accessibility features and apps that don't, and while you may not *need* to support them to be financially successful in the App Store, users who rely on these features will thank you.

Providing Accessibility Labels

To start improving accessibility in TapALap, let's begin with the Go Running screen. This is the first screen new users will see, so it's important to make it work well. The Selected Track and Start Run buttons both sound right, but the groups at the bottom could use some work. Each label is spoken individually by VoiceOver. Not ideal. Let's start with the Average Pace label. While this label is not actually filled in with our real run data, we know that the "9:12" represents an average pace of 9 minutes and 12 seconds. What you need to do is to tell VoiceOver to say *that* instead. To do this, you'll specify an *accessibility label* for the label.

Accessibility labels, as well as other accessibility-related properties you're going to use, are defined on WKInterfaceObject, from which all interface objects inherit. To set an accessibility label on an interface object, it's as simple as calling setAccessibilityLabel(_:) with the text you'd like VoiceOver to read. For this case, you can also set the text in the storyboard. Open up Interface.storyboard and select the 9:12 label in the Go Running interface controller. Unlike most other interface object properties that you set using the Attributes Inspector, accessibility information is set using the Identity Inspector. Open the inspector with ⌘⌥3 and you'll see the accessibility information at the bottom of the inspector. Enter "9 minutes, 12 seconds" for the accessibility label; then rerun the app using VoiceOver. Much better!

What makes a good accessibility label? Be sure not to include identifying words like "button"—watchOS will add them when necessary. The label should speak the *content* of the element to the user. Most of the time such words are unnecessary, but anytime text in an element is abbreviated, incomplete, or cropped to fit the small size of the watch face, use the full text for the accessibility label. If you're using an NSFormatter, it's a good idea to have two formatters: one for the interface text, one for the accessibility label. Actually implementing the Average Pace label is an exercise left to the reader, but it would look something like this:

```
func updateAveragePaceLabel(averagePace: NSTimeInterval) {
    let labelTextFormatter = NSDateComponentsFormatter()
    let labelAccessibilityLabelFormatter = NSDateComponentsFormatter()

    labelTextFormatter.allowedUnits = [.Minute, .Second]
    labelAccessibilityLabelFormatter.allowedUnits = [.Minute, .Second]

    labelTextFormatter.unitsStyle = .Positional
    labelAccessibilityLabelFormatter.unitsStyle = .SpellOut

    averagePaceLabel.setText(
        labelTextFormatter.stringFromTimeInterval(averagePace))

    averagePaceLabel.setAccessibilityLabel(
        labelAccessibilityLabelFormatter.stringFromTimeInterval(averagePace))
}
```

In this example, we create two NSDateComponentsFormatter instances: one to use the .Positional units style, which formats our pace as "9:12," and one to use the .SpellOut units style, which formats our pace as "nine minutes, twelve seconds." While this method of handling the average pace requires us to duplicate some work, it's pretty simple once the code is there. The only problem with this part of the screen now is that the Runs and Average Pace labels below their respective values don't really add much value to the screen. It would be better if the two sets of labels could be read together—instead of "5," "runs," "nine minutes, twelve seconds," and finally "average pace," it would be nice if our users would just hear the two data points: "5 runs" and "nine minutes, twelve seconds average pace." Let's look at how to accomplish that next.

Using Accessibility Elements to Group Objects

Both of the labels for statistics on this screen are in a group with a caption label underneath. Conceptually, to a VoiceOver user, the *group* is one thing: on the left, the number of runs, and on the right, their average pace. The fact that we've split out the data and the captions inside groups really doesn't matter to VoiceOver users. To achieve this, you'll set the groups as *accessibility elements*, which tells watchOS to treat them as a single unit of content. Let's set this up to see how it works.

Open the watch app storyboard and select the groups. In the Identity Inspector, you'll notice the accessibility options we were using before don't appear. By default, groups are not accessibility elements—they're invisible to the VoiceOver system. Select Disabled and enable the groups, as in this screenshot:

Build and run again, and move your finger over the groups. Now, instead of speaking the content of the individual labels, VoiceOver speaks the content of the groups all at once. Marking an interface object as an accessibility element causes VoiceOver to speak its contents; just as you can enable accessibility for a group to read the group's contents, you can *disable* it for any other element to cause VoiceOver to skip it. This is perfect for images and text content that are for decoration only. You can do this in code, too; simply call setIsAccessibilityElement(_:) on an interface object to change the value.

Accessibility labels and elements are great for reading your content, but what about the Selected Track button? For a VoiceOver user, it might not be obvious that this is the button they need to press in order to select a track. Let's help them out and give them some more information.

Providing Accessibility Hints

When you select a button with VoiceOver, you'll hear the system speak the word "button" after it reads the label. Your Go Running interface controller has two buttons: Selected Track and Start Run. While the Start Run button is fairly self-explanatory, it may not be immediately obvious to the user that they should tap Selected Track to select a new track. You use the chevron graphic to try to indicate this for sighted users, but for VoiceOver users, you can do even better.

In the storyboard, select the Selected Track button and open the Identity Inspector to change accessibility settings. The item you're interested in is Hint. The hint should describe to the user what happens when she selects the button. For this button, set the hint to "Tap to select a track." Build and run, and then navigate to the button in VoiceOver. You'll hear something like this: "Selected track. None. Button," and then, after a short delay, "Tap to select a track." The hint allows you to give some extra contextual information to the button that can really help users understand the behavior of your app. Of course, you can also set the hint in code, using setAccessibilityHint(_:) on any WKInterfaceObject subclass.

Describing Images with Image Regions

While all of these examples are great for built-in controls, sometimes a complicated layout in your interface needs a little more help. If you're using images with multiple pieces of data in them, having VoiceOver read the entire image's accessibility label might not be what you want. For more complicated image-based layouts, WatchKit has one more API to help VoiceOver users get the most out of your apps: *image regions*. Image regions allow you to break an image into multiple pieces, with each piece having its own accessibility information. If you have, say, an image of a pizza where each half has different toppings, image regions are a great choice to break that up. If you did any web development in the dark days before CSS, you may remember the technique of image maps[1] to split an image into multiple clickable regions. Image regions in WatchKit are similar.

Image regions are defined in the context of the source image. If you have an image of a pizza that's 200 pixels square, you'd define the regions of the image as shown here:

```
let firstHalfFrame = CGRect(x: 0, y: 0, width: 100, height: 200)
let secondHalfFrame = CGRect(x: 100, y: 0, width: 100, height: 200)
```

---

1. https://en.wikipedia.org/wiki/Image_map

The frames of the accessibility regions are in the coordinate system of the image you're labeling. Once you have the frame, you create WKAccessibilityImageRegion instances and set two values: their frame and the label to speak when they're active:

```
let firstRegion = WKAccessibilityImageRegion()
firstRegion.frame = firstHalfFrame
firstRegion.label = "First Half: Pepperoni, Onions, and Mushroom"

let secondRegion = WKAccessibilityImageRegion()
secondRegion.frame = secondHalfFrame
secondRegion.label = "Second Half: Pepperoni"
```

This code sets up two regions, one for the pizza half with onions and mushroom, and one without. Finally, the last step is to add the accessibility regions to the image:

```
pizzaImage.setAccessibilityImageRegions([firstRegion, secondRegion])
```

Just like that, an image is better for a VoiceOver user: she can move her finger across it to "read" the regions. While not every image needs accessibility regions, they're a great way to enable VoiceOver users to get complicated information from your UI.

Not only do these enhancements you've made to TapALap in the name of supporting accessibility help VoiceOver users with the app, but they also help you think about the structure of the app in new ways. An app that's clear, simple, and easy to use for one user should be the same for all users. Continually testing your apps with VoiceOver and other accessibility features enabled is a great way to think about their structure in new ways.

Wrap-Up

Your app is now ready for the big stage. You support all sorts of users around the globe, regardless of the language they speak or their abilities. All that's left is to put it on the App Store and wait for the Apple checks to roll in, right? Not exactly. As anyone who's been involved in the app ecosystem will tell you, finishing this book (and, by extension, your app) is just the beginning. Once an app is released, it needs support, marketing, and regular updates to become a commercial success. Becoming a good citizen and supporting as many users as possible helps, but it's up to you to make the best app you can. Good luck!

Index

More on iOS

Get up to speed on the latest in iOS 9 and Core Data using Swift.

iOS 9 SDK Development

iOS 9 gives developers new tools for creating apps for iPhone and iPad, and our new edition of the classic iOS guide is updated to match. By writing clean, expressive, and maintainable Swift code, you

Chris Adamson with Janie Clayton
(342 pages) ISBN: 9781680501322. $42
https://pragprog.com/book/adios3

Core Data in Swift

Core Data is intricate, powerful, and necessary. Discover the powerful capabilities integrated into Core Data, and how to use Core Data in your iOS and OS X projects. All examples are current for OS X El Capitan, iOS 9, and the latest release of Core Data. All the code is written in Swift, including numerous examples of how best to integrate Core Data with Apple's newest programming language.

Marcus S. Zarra
(250 pages) ISBN: 9781680501704. $38
https://pragprog.com/book/mzswift

Exercises and Teams

From exercises to make you a better programmer to techniques for creating better teams, we've got you covered.

Exercises for Programmers

When you write software, you need to be at the top of your game. Great programmers practice to keep their skills sharp. Get sharp and stay sharp with more than fifty practice exercises rooted in real-world scenarios. If you're a new programmer, these challenges will help you learn what you need to break into the field, and if you're a seasoned pro, you can use these exercises to learn that hot new language for your next gig.

Brian P. Hogan
(118 pages) ISBN: 9781680501223. $24
https://pragprog.com/book/bhwb

Creating Great Teams

People are happiest and most productive if they can choose what they work on and who they work with. Self-selecting teams give people that choice. Build well-designed and efficient teams to get the most out of your organization, with step-by-step instructions on how to set up teams quickly and efficiently. You'll create a process that works for you, whether you need to form teams from scratch, improve the design of existing teams, or are on the verge of a big team re-shuffle.

Sandy Mamoli and David Mole
(102 pages) ISBN: 9781680501285. $17
https://pragprog.com/book/mmteams

The Joy of Mazes and Math

Rediscover the joy and fascinating weirdness of mazes and pure mathematics.

Mazes for Programmers

A book on mazes? Seriously?

Yes!

Not because you spend your day creating mazes, or because you particularly like solving mazes.

But because it's fun. Remember when programming used to be fun? This book takes you back to those days when you were starting to program, and you wanted to make your code do things, draw things, and solve puzzles. It's fun because it lets you explore and grow your code, and reminds you how it feels to just think.

Sometimes it feels like you live your life in a maze of twisty little passages, all alike. Now you can code your way out.

Jamis Buck
(286 pages) ISBN: 9781680500554. $38
https://pragprog.com/book/jbmaze

Good Math

Mathematics is beautiful—and it can be fun and exciting as well as practical. *Good Math* is your guide to some of the most intriguing topics from two thousand years of mathematics: from Egyptian fractions to Turing machines; from the real meaning of numbers to proof trees, group symmetry, and mechanical computation. If you've ever wondered what lay beyond the proofs you struggled to complete in high school geometry, or what limits the capabilities of the computer on your desk, this is the book for you.

Mark C. Chu-Carroll
(282 pages) ISBN: 9781937785338. $34
https://pragprog.com/book/mcmath

Past and Present

To see where we're going, remember how we got here, and learn how to take a healthier approach to programming.

Fire in the Valley

In the 1970s, while their contemporaries were protesting the computer as a tool of dehumanization and oppression, a motley collection of college dropouts, hippies, and electronics fanatics were engaged in something much more subversive. Obsessed with the idea of getting computer power into their own hands, they launched from their garages a hobbyist movement that grew into an industry, and ultimately a social and technological revolution. What they did was invent the personal computer: not just a new device, but a watershed in the relationship between man and machine. This is their story.

Michael Swaine and Paul Freiberger
(424 pages) ISBN: 9781937785765. $34
https://pragprog.com/book/fsfire

The Healthy Programmer

To keep doing what you love, you need to maintain your own systems, not just the ones you write code for. Regular exercise and proper nutrition help you learn, remember, concentrate, and be creative—skills critical to doing your job well. Learn how to change your work habits, master exercises that make working at a computer more comfortable, and develop a plan to keep fit, healthy, and sharp for years to come.

This book is intended only as an informative guide for those wishing to know more about health issues. In no way is this book intended to replace, countermand, or conflict with the advice given to you by your own healthcare provider including Physician, Nurse Practitioner, Physician Assistant, Registered Dietician, and other licensed professionals.

Joe Kutner
(254 pages) ISBN: 9781937785314. $36
https://pragprog.com/book/jkthp

Seven in Seven

From Web Frameworks to Concurrency Models, see what the rest of the world is doing with this introduction to seven different approaches.

Seven Web Frameworks in Seven Weeks

Whether you need a new tool or just inspiration, *Seven Web Frameworks in Seven Weeks* explores modern options, giving you a taste of each with ideas that will help you create better apps. You'll see frameworks that leverage modern programming languages, employ unique architectures, live client-side instead of server-side, or embrace type systems. You'll see everything from familiar Ruby and JavaScript to the more exotic Erlang, Haskell, and Clojure.

Jack Moffitt, Fred Daoud
(302 pages) ISBN: 9781937785635. $38
https://pragprog.com/book/7web

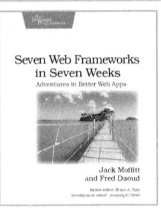

Seven Concurrency Models in Seven Weeks

Your software needs to leverage multiple cores, handle thousands of users and terabytes of data, and continue working in the face of both hardware and software failure. Concurrency and parallelism are the keys, and *Seven Concurrency Models in Seven Weeks* equips you for this new world. See how emerging technologies such as actors and functional programming address issues with traditional threads and locks development. Learn how to exploit the parallelism in your computer's GPU and leverage clusters of machines with MapReduce and Stream Processing. And do it all with the confidence that comes from using tools that help you write crystal clear, high-quality code.

Paul Butcher
(296 pages) ISBN: 9781937785659. $38
https://pragprog.com/book/pb7con

More Seven in Seven

You need to learn at least one new language every year. Here are fourteen excellent suggestions to get started.

Seven Languages in Seven Weeks

You should learn a programming language every year, as recommended by *The Pragmatic Programmer*. But if one per year is good, how about *Seven Languages in Seven Weeks*? In this book you'll get a hands-on tour of Clojure, Haskell, Io, Prolog, Scala, Erlang, and Ruby. Whether or not your favorite language is on that list, you'll broaden your perspective of programming by examining these languages side-by-side. You'll learn something new from each, and best of all, you'll learn how to learn a language quickly.

Bruce A. Tate
(330 pages) ISBN: 9781934356593. $34.95
https://pragprog.com/book/btlang

Seven More Languages in Seven Weeks

Great programmers aren't born—they're made. The industry is moving from object-oriented languages to functional languages, and you need to commit to radical improvement. New programming languages arm you with the tools and idioms you need to refine your craft. While other language primers take you through basic installation and "Hello, World," we aim higher. Each language in *Seven More Languages in Seven Weeks* will take you on a step-by-step journey through the most important paradigms of our time. You'll learn seven exciting languages: Lua, Factor, Elixir, Elm, Julia, MiniKanren, and Idris.

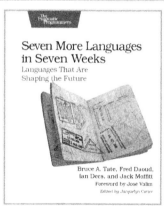

Bruce Tate, Fred Daoud, Jack Moffitt, Ian Dees
(318 pages) ISBN: 9781941222157. $38
https://pragprog.com/book/7lang

The Pragmatic Bookshelf

The Pragmatic Bookshelf features books written by developers for developers. The titles continue the well-known Pragmatic Programmer style and continue to garner awards and rave reviews. As development gets more and more difficult, the Pragmatic Programmers will be there with more titles and products to help you stay on top of your game.

Visit Us Online

This Book's Home Page
https://pragprog.com/book/jkwatch2
Source code from this book, errata, and other resources. Come give us feedback, too!

Register for Updates
https://pragprog.com/updates
Be notified when updates and new books become available.

Join the Community
https://pragprog.com/community
Read our weblogs, join our online discussions, participate in our mailing list, interact with our wiki, and benefit from the experience of other Pragmatic Programmers.

New and Noteworthy
https://pragprog.com/news
Check out the latest pragmatic developments, new titles and other offerings.

Save on the eBook

Save on the eBook versions of this title. Owning the paper version of this book entitles you to purchase the electronic versions at a terrific discount.

PDFs are great for carrying around on your laptop—they are hyperlinked, have color, and are fully searchable. Most titles are also available for the iPhone and iPod touch, Amazon Kindle, and other popular e-book readers.

Buy now at *https://pragprog.com/coupon*

Contact Us

Online Orders: *https://pragprog.com/catalog*
Customer Service: *support@pragprog.com*
International Rights: *translations@pragprog.com*
Academic Use: *academic@pragprog.com*
Write for Us: *http://write-for-us.pragprog.com*
Or Call: +1 800-699-7764

CPSIA information can be obtained at www.ICGtesting.com
Printed in the USA
BVOW09s1725110516

447650BV00003B/4/P

9 781680 501339